HERE
COMES
LIFE!◆

Seeking Wholeness and Happiness

JIM CLARKE

FOREWORD BY
Thomas P. Rausch, SJ

Paulist Press
New York / Mahwah, NJ

Scripture texts in this work are taken from the New American Bible, revised edition © 2010, 1991, 1986, 1970 Confraternity of Christian Doctrine, Washington, D.C. and are used by permission of the copyright owner. All Rights Reserved. No part of the New American Bible may be reproduced in any form without permission in writing from the copyright owner.

Cover image by echo3005/Shutterstock.com
Cover and book design by Lynn Else

Copyright © 2021 by James Clarke

All rights reserved. No part of this publication may be reproduced, stored in a retrieval system, or transmitted in any form or by any means, electronic, mechanical, photocopying, recording, scanning, or otherwise, without either the prior written permission of the Publisher, or authorization through payment of the appropriate per-copy fee to the Copyright Clearance Center, Inc., www.copyright.com. Requests to the Publisher for permission should be addressed to the Permissions Department, Paulist Press, permissions@paulistpress.com.

Library of Congress Cataloging-in-Publication Data
Names: Clarke, Jim (James J.), author
Title: Here comes life! : seeking wholeness and happiness / Jim Clarke.
Description: New York/Mahwah : Paulist Press, 2021. | Summary: "Here Comes Life!-with all its questions, longings, challenges, and mis-steps; but even more importantly, with its constant search for wholeness and happiness. It is not concerned with canonical or theological debates, but with pastoral considerations. Here Comes Life! shows the reader how to live out the teachings of Pope Francis in real life"—Provided by publisher.
Identifiers: LCCN 2020006681 (print) | LCCN 2020006682 (ebook) | ISBN 9780809155125 (paperback) | ISBN 9781587689116 (ebook)
Subjects: LCSH: Christian life—Catholic authors. | Francis, Pope, 1936–
Classification: LCC BX2350.3 .C575 2021 (print) | LCC BX2350.3 (ebook) | DDC 248.4—dc23
LC record available at https://lccn.loc.gov/2020006681
LC ebook record available at https://lccn.loc.gov/2020006682

ISBN 978-0-8091-5512-5 (paperback)
ISBN 978-1-58768-911-6 (e-book)

Published by Paulist Press
997 Macarthur Boulevard
Mahwah, New Jersey 07430
www.paulistpress.com

Printed and bound in the
United States of America

To those who struggle with their faith, who wrestle with the deeper questions of life, and to the indomitable women who continue to believe that one day their Church will believe in, and embrace, the fullness of their humanity

CONTENTS

CONTENTS

FOREWORD

WHEN I ASK my undergraduate students a question about God, Jesus, or the Church, they often respond with a dismissive, "I'm not religious," which, for them, means the end of the conversation. Though most are willing to give me a hearing, few practice their faith, while many more grew up without a religious tradition. They are among the "nones," those without a religious affiliation who today make up 36 percent of our young people. But losses include more than the young. Catholics have dropped from 23 percent of the population in 2009 to 20 percent today.

A recent study of disaffiliated young adults by Saint Mary's Press is entitled, *Going, Going, Gone*. Many find reasons to drop out, or simply stop believing. Some feel injured by the loss of a loved one or a family crisis such as a divorce. Some simply drift away, lacking religious support from family, friends, or a faith community. Usually their parents are not practicing, as they tell me in their religious autobiographies, always my first assignment. One said plaintively, "I wish my parents had been religious; maybe I'd have some religion myself." Faith is not easy today. We live in a secular age, as Charles Taylor puts it in his massive study of the same title. There are few cultural supports for a life of faith, let alone ecclesial participation.

For many, called by the Saint Mary's study "dissenters," the Church itself is a problem. Young people point to the Church's attitude toward gays or its inability to more adequately recognize the gifts of women. The sexual abuse scandal is now over thirty years old, and though the Church has taken serious steps to address it, these steps are not always recognized and stories about the crisis are still in the headlines. Many find the Church too judgmental, its values out of sync with their own. I hear this frequently. Too many think that being a Christian means joining the religious right.

Still, many young people today are not happy. Suicide is the second leading cause of death among those between the ages of ten and twenty-four. According to the Center for Disease Control and Prevention, the suicide rate for this group increased by 56 percent between 2007 and 2017. At a major California university in 2019, nine students died in less than three months: three by suicide, though the causes of the other deaths have not been disclosed. A dean at the school spoke of a "loneliness crisis." At my university, the counseling department includes a "comfort animal," a friendly labradoodle that students can play with for an hour at a time. It's always busy. During finals week, another department sponsors a petting zoo with dogs, goats, and sheep that stressed students can interact with.

Fr. Jim Clarke's book, *Here Comes Life!*, seeks to open a richer, deeper life for all of us. Teacher, theologian, traveler, and spiritual director, Clarke is most of all a pastor. His book reflects his deep humanity, his pastoral experience, his spirituality. Full of stories of ordinary people, not perfect but good, men and women trying to live lives of faith; it is a wisdom book. Much of it comes from his long experience as a teacher, spiritual director, and giver of retreats to diverse groups. His students value his courses.

He takes up issues that all of us struggle with. How do we deal with children whose choices we question? How do we develop more inclusive hearts? Does our faith deepen our humanity? What are our spiritual practices and does our eucharistic participation shape our daily lives? Have we experienced the "ecological conversion" called for by Pope Francis? He argues that our faith is never simply private, for it is always lived out in community and it is there that we learn to love. An adult faith is not incompatible with questioning religious authority, even official teachings. Women especially are impatient with black-and-white answers. They know they rarely work. They have learned to be comfortable with nuance.

Fr. Clarke probes feelings many of us experience, feelings of hurt or anger or resentment, drawing on Scripture or the lives of the saints to help us find meaning in them. His book is always practical. Like the good spiritual director that he is, he offers concrete suggestions for moving beyond our negative feelings. Using the imagination can be a help. One chapter offers suggestions for developing a healthy masculinity, getting men in touch with their interior lives, to develop a spirituality that is authentically masculine. Retreats are an important aid to this; so is service that touches something deep within the male psyche.

Another chapter on forgiveness is especially helpful. How do we forgive others, even God? He writes, to "choose not to forgive is like drinking poison and hoping the other person will die." Forgiveness is never easy and cannot be rushed. It does not mean that we forget. It demands prayer and often ritual expression. I may not be able to change the other, but I can change myself.

Clarke is honest about the Church, with all its shortcomings and sins. Its flawed humanity is all too evident. He says the Church is messy because our lives are messy. But his love for the Church shines through. The Church is a mystery; it helps us come to know the unknowable God. It opens us to God's life with symbols rich and nourishing. It proclaims the gospel that continues to call us to live more generous lives and gives us holy men and women as companions on the way. It is a Church learning to be more inclusive, to be a place of grace and succor and support for those who struggle and search for the divine, trying to do their best. At its best, its teachers and ministers can offer guiding principles, realizing that one size does not fit all.

The book reads like an honest conversation with a good friend. Our images of God often change as we struggle with questions of faith. Clarke compares faith to a living tree, growing upward and downward, deepening and broadening us. He counsels patience, like Pope Francis, who tells us that experience is more important than ideas, and that growth is a process; it demands time. One chapter charts how his own siblings and their children have gone in different directions, like so many of our own.

Some will find the book controversial. Always he asks, how do we connect with God, and recognize where the Lord is calling us at this moment? This may mean questioning authority while remaining faithful, or learning to recognize that morality is more than rules, or respecting others who make different choices, even when they are in our own families. We need to learn that sexuality remains a mystery, part of God's plan to bring us into deeper communion with another. Clarke has a profound respect for the mystery of each person. His concern is to develop an adult spirituality, aware that each of us must find our own way to God. The stories he tells are full of insight for those still on the way.

Thomas P. Rausch, SJ
Emeritus T. Marie Chilton Professor of Catholic Theology
Loyola Marymount University

PREFACE

LIFE IS MESSY and complicated. Being a Catholic in today's world is no longer a life of comfort and security. The path to heaven is not as clear-cut as it used to be. This book is about my privileged immersion into the lives of ordinary people around the world who graced me with their questions, their pushbacks, their stories of suffering, but most of all, their faith. They have expanded the boundaries of my white, middle-class, orthodox thinking. They have challenged my certainty about my theological stances, and they have invited me into a more thoroughly incarnational way of thinking.

The two great passions of my ministry are spiritual direction and teaching. The life's work of a theology teacher always is to bring theological concepts into the heart of people's lives in a practical way that is not only challenging and confronting but also reassuring, comforting, and, most importantly, life-giving. Pope Francis has focused on this aspect of pastoral theology in very creative ways like symbolic gestures and metaphors that invite people to think more deeply about the meaning of being human. As a Senior Lecturer at Loyola Marymount University in Los Angeles and former Director of Spiritual Formation at St. John's Seminary in Camarillo, California, my aim has been always to bring the ethereal to the material, and vice versa, with both my current and former students. I have always been fascinated by the ideals of our faith, but I have learned the necessity of bringing these ideals to the unpredictability of my own and others' lives.

At heart, I am a pastor, but I am of the Pauline variety rather than the more common Petrine expression of priesthood. The call of the people of God, as my ministerial life has evolved, has come from diverse and scattered communities of people, although I remain faithful to my commitment as a diocesan priest of the Archdiocese of Los Angeles. Reflecting on forty years of active ordained ministry, I have concluded that this is truly my vocation—to go where I am invited to proclaim the good news of the kingdom of God. What a privilege!

Specialist ministry assignments have enabled me to engage in what I would call extracurricular ministerial opportunities, thus I have been invited to preach retreats to priests, women religious, permanent deacons and their wives, lay leaders, and ordinary men and women around the world. I have also led parish missions and pilgrimages to many of the holy sites in Europe and the Middle East. One of the most exciting and energizing areas of my work has been the facilitating of Men's Rites of Passage retreat experiences, originally with Fr. Richard Rohr, OFM, and now with Illuman, an international men's organization.

Over the years, I have had the privilege of living and working in suburban as well as inner-city parishes, always with multicultural populations; this has allowed me to expand my cultural horizons. Learning Spanish and Mexican culture

Preface

in Mexico during my years of seminary formation opened another door for me that allowed me to communicate the good news to another important group of people—our Latino brothers and sisters. At present, I serve as the director of new evangelization for the Archdiocese of Los Angeles, charged with the responsibility of consulting with the pastoral leadership of many parishes in discerning the best ways to share the good news with the people of God.

This book is not concerned with canonical matters, nor does it concern itself with abstruse theological debates; it is not didactic in nature. It is purely and simply concerned with pastoral considerations, and it has, I hope, "the smell of the sheep." All conversations, questions, and wonderings recorded in the pages of this book come from genuine pastoral encounters with real people who shared their life experiences with me in a spirit of trust and openness. In some cases, names have been changed to protect privacy.

Here Comes Life—with all its questions, longings, challenges, and missteps; but even more importantly, with its constant search for wholeness and happiness.

Here's to Life!

ACKNOWLEDGMENTS

THANKS TO ALL those who were willing to share their stories, their moral dilemmas, and their experience of both the presence and the absence of God in their lives.

Chapter 1
NO, IT'S NOT ALL OK!

THE LOFOTEN ISLANDS lie above the Arctic Circle, off the northern coast of Norway. Encompassing a small scattering of verdant hillsides, rocky shores, and several lovely beaches, these sparsely populated beauty spots are home to the fishermen and their families who inhabit small, colorful villages strung through the archipelago. The islands regularly enjoy the benefit of a warm ocean current, which sustains the rich fishing grounds and intermittently blesses the islands with pleasant, balmy weather.

Three years ago, traveling with a group through Norway, I found myself in this strangely beautiful place. The day was sunny and warm enough that people swam or played beach volleyball—yes, above the Arctic Circle! One in our party, Catherine, a highly educated Catholic woman who knew I was a priest, asked if she could join me on a walk along the beach—a good opportunity for a private conversation.

Catherine had, she said with some asperity, some questions for me. And I knew it was not going to be a conversation about Mass times.

Like many in her generation, Catherine grew up believing and accepting everything that the Church taught, with little questioning of its authority. As she matured in age, she found that her spirituality did not keep pace with the growing complexities of her life. Thus began her inner turmoil. We all know, from personal and communal experience, that life is messy and complicated; it can rarely be reduced to a clear-cut set of choices. Most of life is situated in that vast gray area that bridges the extremes of absolute certainty and total confusion. This inevitably raises all sorts of questions for those seeking a strict delineation of sin and holiness. In reality, most human situations straddle these concepts. For this reason, we must develop mature ways of dealing with the realities of life, marriage, family, and our own participation in societal relationships. Pope Francis's memorable line, "Who am I to judge?," while not definitive for morality, gives us a healthy reminder of the ambiguities we must deal with. All of us have made "dodgy" choices at one time or another and been forced to live with the consequences. We also know family members and friends who have done the same thing.

My spirituality and my moral response need to match the incongruities of my life; otherwise, faith is meaningless and out of touch. A mature human being directly engages the mysteries, paradoxes, and contradictions of life, seeking greater fulfillment and meaning. The Church, at its best, invites us to fully participate in this ongoing work so that we might move from a childish allegiance to authority to a personal adult faith. This is best imaged in the Hebrew Scriptures as Yahweh walking and growing with God's people. This is a mutual collaborative work.

God is our partner in life, and we are God's partners in God's life.

Catherine shared that, like many faith-filled believers, she found herself in conflict with a full range of Church teachings in the personal morality arena. I listened attentively as she ticked off a brief list of these teachings. "Why," she complained, "does the Church still insist that artificial contraception is morally wrong, when it is an established fact that most faithful Catholic women are using it and remain at ease in their spiritual life?" At its core, this Catholic teaching is about avoiding a "contraceptive mentality" toward human sexuality, regarding it only as a source for human pleasure with no responsible interaction or aftermath. Whenever human beings are engaged in any form of activity, especially intimate behavior, responsible choices and decisions must be made for the good of *all* persons involved both in the present and for the future. This holistic approach honors the whole person and situation as a means to participate more fully in the co-creative, collaborative work with the Creator. What is best for the couple not only in this particular moment of desire but for the future of their relationship and the community to which they belong? There is no such thing as a private act of morality. All moral acts have public consequences and therefore necessitate responsible decision-making.

This teaching of the Church is not dogmatic; rather it comes from a Pastoral Encyclical entitled *Humanae Vitae*, which carries a lesser form of authority. It falls under the category of an exhortation that expects a modicum of respect and reflection upon the theme being addressed. It invites every believer to reflect upon the question, How can I best create something new through my humanity? How am I able to allow the flow of life and love to work through me? Then, from this point of view, what type of discipline will aid this process? The choice of when, where, and how to make love, with its possible consequences, then flow from this reflective work. We are meant to engage the wisdom of this document in such a way that it opens us up to a larger perspective of human sexuality and enhances a mature, religious response.

There are numerous rulings in Scripture that reflect the social conventions of their time and are thus open to change: for example, animal sacrifice, skin diseases, Sabbath requirements. Like all legislation, canon law is changeable. The judgment on which laws are absolute and essential to the Christian message and which are relative to times and context of their elaboration is deferred to canon lawyers. As Catholics, we believe in a hierarchy of values—some things are more important than others. This is true in theology, Scripture, morality, canon law, Church teachings, and ministry. This is why we have experts in each of these fields to remind us of what is most important. The danger comes when we get these layers of importance mixed up or confused. Think of Jesus's admonition in Matthew 23:23–24: "You pay tithes of mint and dill and cummin, and have neglected the weightier things of the law: judgment and mercy and fidelity. [But] these you should have done, without neglecting the others. Blind guides, who strain out the gnat and swallow the camel!"

Another important component of Catherine's inner conflict is the peace she experiences in her spiritual life and her prayer, despite not following the Church's teaching on this aspect of contraception. As I have said elsewhere and will say again, this is not unusual. At its best, the Church points us in the right direction toward God. As adults, each of us must find our own way on this journey to God. This involves a path of discerning and choosing what works for us at each stage of our journey. This is one reason why the Church has a long and revered tradition of spiritual direction and pastoral counseling for its members. Advances in scientific understanding should be matched by the integrity of our theological perception coupled with our own imaginal creativity. This is the real work of mature integration and discernment of God's will in any circumstance. An informed conscience is one that is cognizant of and respects the teaching of the Church and proceeds with logic and reason to guide our actions. A well-formed conscience can help guide a person to make the right moral and ethical choices in life (*Catechism of the Catholic Church* 1777, 1783, 1785). Talking through the details of our lives, trying to discern God's will and what is best for us in each situation, is a real challenge. Like Jesus (Luke 2:40), we must grow into wholeness; it is not given to us all at once in a rush of spiritual enthusiasm. Often we move from one growth spurt to another. The peace or relative "ease" that Catherine experiences is a sign of "restful accomplishment" that is finished for now but continues with the next opportunity.

Catherine went on to mention that her eldest daughter is a lesbian in a committed, loving relationship that has all the hallmarks of the sacramental nature of a blessed lifelong partnership:

- Permanence
- Mutuality
- Equality
- Fidelity
- Openness to life

Their love for each other flows into the larger family, blessing their nieces and nephews, as well as their siblings, in a way that is different but nonetheless life-giving. The Church worries that gay marriage will destroy sacramental marriage, but this mother sees the opposite happening. She sees the marital love of all her children being enhanced and honored in the large family setting.

Sexual activity is a choice, but sexual identity is an orientation. Human sexuality is a mystery to be pondered and respected. Social sciences tell us that it is best understood as a continuum. The Church offers ideals to work toward, for each of us, as we wrestle with the complex reality of our lives and of our loved ones. As we read the Scriptures and reflect upon Church history, we note that there have always been norms to guide us in living a good moral life. But right behind the norms there also have been exceptions. Is it possible that in this particular area of human sexuality, we are dealing with the exceptions to the norm? What then? It certainly changes our dogmatic stance and moves us to a place of greater humility and more careful and respectful dialogue with the social sciences of our present time in human history.

Catherine also shared that her two adult sons lived with their girlfriends before they were married—certainly not an uncommon phenomenon these days in Catholic families. In this type of situation, it is best to focus on what is most important, and that is right relationship. How easy it is to judge or condemn someone else for their moral failures and to let ourselves off the hook. A better way to approach this dilemma is to stand back and look at the bigger picture. Social scientists point out that in Western society more than 70 percent of couples have had an active sexual relationship with their proposed spouse before marriage. What is happening as a result of this sexualized relationship? Is there a greater growth in self-knowledge and relational maturity? A more realistic view of marriage with this person? This is what caused the conflict for Catherine—she noticed that her sons seemed to mature and "grow into" marriage—and yet their life choice conflicted with Church teaching. Ideals are to be striven for, but not slavishly obeyed without some real interactive participation at a deeper level. This is what it means to be "formed." For God meets us in the messy details of our lives—grace impacting our nature and environment! Growth is unique to each individual. No one pathway fits every person's needs at the same time. We each must find our own way with the guidance of the Great Tradition. This is where the Church fits in. At its best, the Church offers us guiding principles to accompany us on our evolving journey to become our best selves. One size does not fit all; we each must find what enables and supports our own growth in human wholeness. This is why we are told not to judge or condemn others who are struggling to discern their path. Real evil must be confronted and condemned, but that is not what we are talking about here.

The fact is, God meets us where we struggle the most. For some people, this is in the area of authority issues, for others it is around deceit, still others—sexuality, or power, or money issues. Each arena of life opens possibilities for us to move toward a greater fullness of our humanity.

Perhaps the greatest angst that Catherine faces at this point in her life is the question that has often been put to her by her middle-aged brothers and other friends: "How can an intelligent and informed woman like you remain in the Catholic Church?" Only she can answer this query to the satisfaction of her own integrity. But I would add these thoughts: The Church, like all human institutions, is incomplete, and often fails to live up to its stated values. This does not mean that we stop practicing the values that we stand for. The best response is not the removal from the scene of this disparity in stated values and lived reality; rather it is the continuing practice of the good in the face of perceived blindness, contradictions, or injustice.

Wherever human beings come together—in family, in community, in the church, or in government—these imperfections will be present. The challenge, and the call, is for a mature, informed, adult response that is faithful to the great traditions of justice, mercy, and integrity that mark Christianity at its best.

As we reached the far end of the beach and turned to retrace our steps, I noticed something I had not seen earlier: On the high peak of a nearby mountain, sprouted a forest of steel towers, antennae, and dish antennae. Incongruent in this beautiful and remote setting, but clearly erected to listen to distant communications, to capture ideas, conversations, perhaps orders, across the top of the world.

We, too, need to walk in a combination of the quiet beauty of our human being, but equipped with an alert listening post tuned to the sometimes distant, but always faintly audible, voice of the spirit coming to us as we discern our true path homeward. Like the isolated, lonely islands of the Lofoten archipelago, we hold to our beauty and our serenity, and wait for the warm currents of God's love and fidelity to carry us through the winters of our discontent.

Chapter 2

WHATEVER HAPPENED TO MY CHURCH?

I GREW UP in Lawndale, California, in a suburban tract home that was part of the postwar housing boom. My father was a World War II GI, and like many other veterans, his longing was for safe, comfortable suburbia, surrounded by people like himself. Family was very important as were friends and community, but most of all, parish. The parish was the place where he experienced acceptance, understanding, and affirmation. Daily Mass was the glue that bound him to his peers. There was an unwritten set of rules, and many assumed that things would go on like this forever. Dad was fully involved in the life of the parish—lector, prayer group leader, parish council representative, daily communicant. He had spent five years in the seminary and my Mom had been in the convent for two and a half years. Dad knew the parish priests from his seminary days and felt close to them. My mother, needless to say, felt embraced by, and at home in, the parish community. God was in his heaven and all was well with the world.

However, it is the nature of things that nothing can remain the same forever, and this was true in the life of my parents, their community, and their parish.

Right across the street from St. Joseph's Church in Hawthorne, California, stands the venerable establishment of Chips Coffee Shop. Built back in the 1950s, it has the down-home feel of a gathering place for locals, and so it has been, for many years, the after-weekday Mass venue for daily communicants at St. Joseph's. These are older parishioners who have a long history with the parish and with each other. They come to share their sorrows, their struggles, and their wonderings about the future of the parish. Discussions range over parish finances, alienation of the youth, the influx of a growing immigrant population, and the straining of ministerial capacity to meet the growing needs of an increasingly diverse parish.

My parents enjoyed the liveliness of the parish and found the camaraderie and the conversation at Chips to be supportive—even life-giving. My mom and dad lived out of a strong ecclesial nostalgia. They both grew up in deeply devotional families and carried on this tradition by reciting the Morning Office (traditional Scriptural prayers of the Church) together, praying the Rosary, and going to daily Eucharist. They understood the parish as their home and "Father" as the ultimate authority in all matters moral and spiritual.

In 1970 came a watershed moment in their lives when they experienced the "Baptism of the Spirit" through the Charismatic Renewal. Thus began their tentative steps into trusting their own inner authority. This is the long road to spiritual maturity that is now being articulated more clearly by Pope Francis. They started to understand their own responsibility to maturely wrestle with their faith and inform their conscience and to act out of a new notion of Church. My parents brought this new understanding and experience to Chips, and predictably there was a mixed reaction. For some, the old ways were so safe and comfortable that they chose to remain; for others, new possibilities emerged. There was a new sense of the faithful growing, which created an excitement all its own.

Those days of unquestioning faith and practice are irretrievably gone. These folks clung to a culture that was "Cathocentric" in its presentation and practice. This experience of Christendom no longer exists except in the memory of some individuals. In a Church that is polarized in addressing the relationship between immutable, unchangeable doctrine and what is a mature, informed Christ-like response to the North American culture in which we find ourselves, we need to find a deeper wisdom that honors the truth on both sides of the discussion. That truth will only be found in a genuine listening exchange informed by intelligent reading of sources, combined with the lived reality of people's lives. The "old geezers" at Chips would not recognize the discussions we need to have today.

What are some of our urgent questions? What strikes me as fundamental is Pope Francis's call to honor the gospel message above all else—above doctrine, above law, above Church discipline, above Church traditions, above parish concerns, and even above social pressures. He cuts through all our human fears and anxieties to the direct questions of "who are we?" and "where is our center?" Are we inclusive and welcoming of those who are not like us (the "others" of life)? Do we see the parish as a place to receive "spiritual goodies," or do we recognize it as a place for the exchange of life, vitality, and service? We live in a different worldview. How can we maintain a Catholic value system in a world where all parameters have shifted? Perhaps this means that we have to revision what a

Christian community looks like in the twenty-first century. It is no longer limited by parochial boundaries.

For my parents' generation, "tradition," as they understood it, was supremely important. What about for us today? Is it still important? Many people confuse Tradition that dates from the early Church, with traditions that date from the Tridentine period (sixteenth-century issues around liturgy, liturgical dress, clerical authority, etc.). Tradition is not limited to one's favorite religious practices or teachings. It is not about ecclesial nostalgia. Authentic Tradition comes from a wisdom shared by a large faith community gleaned from years of experience and reflection. This living Tradition has long been tested in the fires of persecution and the lived reality of countless saints, mystics, theologians, and artists. History has borne out the truth of what is valuable and lasting and set aside that which is of little use.

When we hold onto traditional religious practices with no concern or acknowledgment of the historical context, then we are dealing with a comfort issue, not an authentic religious commitment. At the heart of religious devotions is the desire to connect with God. This desire can be misdirected if we lose sight of the purpose of devotions—to experience God—and focus only on the form of the devotion itself. For many people, devotions can slip into pride of external practices ("Look what I am doing for God") or superstition (fear of God, rather than experiencing God). This can lead to a multiplicity of prayers, devotions, or practices that hinder, rather than assist, our growth in faith. These phenomena can be found in every culture and can be expressed in extreme practices such as crawling painfully on the ground across jagged stones, self-flagellation, praying one thousand Hail Marys, or fasting from food or sleep for days at a time. Often these well-meaning people have forgotten the purpose of authentic religious prayer or practice—not to gain something from God, but rather to experience God's life and love. Catholic veneration of objects, special places, and individuals is meant to remind us of the invitation to venerate all of creation, beginning with ourselves and extending outward to others. Perhaps this is where proper context can help deliver us from our self-imposed prisons of devotionalism.

And what about "otherness" (one of Pope Francis's favorite topics)? At St. Joseph's Church, parishioners had been told for years by the former pastor that only 10 percent of the parish community was Spanish speaking. Shortly after the new pastor arrived, he was asked to reevaluate and research the accuracy of that estimate. He was stunned when he and the pastoral staff discovered that close to 60 percent of the parishioners spoke Spanish. As a result, in fairness, the pastoral council, along with the pastoral staff, decided to make some courageous decisions that moved the parish to be bilingual in its ministerial offerings and sacramental celebrations. Not everyone was happy, nor was there a full embrace of the new vision. However, it did open the whole question of how to worship and share together the same Catholic faith. The staff came up with some creative ways to respond to this challenge that deepened the bonds of community and helped people to appreciate diverse cultural devotions. It did not always turn out to be a liberating experience for everyone.

I remember the story of an older woman who enjoyed praying "her" Rosary every day no matter the context. One Sunday she positioned herself in the first pew between Masses to pray her Rosary. However, on that day, the first three pews were reserved for the catechumens and candidates preparing to receive their sacraments of initiation. The RCIA director came to tell her this by tapping her lightly on the shoulder and asking her to move to another pew. Without a word, the older woman turned and hit her in the face and went back to praying. In this instance, there definitely was no connection between the prayer and the ensuing action! Prayer and devotions are not meant to be seen or experienced as a duty, but rather as an opportunity to be changed in our relationships with others. It is not about a multiplicity of words, but rather, more importantly, it is meant to be a life-giving, mutual conversation of speaking and listening.

Being part of a larger group of people with similar religious experiences and beliefs strengthens us and keeps us honest in our search for the Reign of God. From the fourth century onward, the Church has borrowed the language of the Roman Empire in naming these groupings: parish, diocese, and basilica. The summary purpose of a parish is to gather a group of people together to regularly worship the Lord and to empower them to serve others in meaningful ways. The parish community reminds us that there is no one way or spirituality to follow Jesus. We all must find the way that works for us.

There seems to be much confusion around our understanding of dogma, doctrine, and the primacy of conscience. Dogma is the core teaching of the Church, summarized in the creedal statements preserved through the centuries. These do not change. Doctrine is the development of these teachings; they change over time with further study and greater insight into the dogmatic teachings (e.g., slavery, the charging of interest on loans, capital punishment). Professor Michael Himes of Boston College puts it this way: all doctrine is salvific; if it does not save, then it is not doctrine. This begs the point that each of us must come to terms with how we interface with these teachings. This is the necessary work of spiritual maturity that translates into coming to terms with change—liturgical changes, cultural shifts, societal changes. Mature faith is always grounded in the present context or reality. It is never removed from the human condition.

Each of us must find our own way to God. The best that the Church can do is point us in the general direction of God. We have the responsibility to live our own lives in truth. The Church will offer us guidelines, but we must balance this outer authority with the inner authority of our own informed conscience (*Catechism of the Catholic Church* 1777–82).

If we have been solidly grounded in an orthodox approach to faith and tradition, then we will tend to progress to a more openhearted expression of that same faith-filled tradition. A personal faith leads a person to an active engagement with the culture. The personal necessarily leads to the communal, as Jesus so eloquently expressed in Matthew 25:31–46: "Amen, I say to you, whatever you did for one of these least brothers of mine, you did for me." Gratitude for our life is meant to be expressed in compassion toward others.

From the Christian perspective, we need to ground our faith in a balanced trinitarian approach. Just as God is a communion of relationships, so are we. We are body, soul, and spirit (1 Thess 5:23–35). Truth resides in all three aspects of our humanity. When we focus only on one or two aspects of our personhood, our lives become like a two-legged stool—it becomes impossible to maintain the balanced tension without falling over. We need to respect all aspects of our life and find ways and means of living a fulfilling life. For this reason, the message of the Scriptures, Tradition, and the Church is both/and: worship *and* service, contemplation *and* action, material *and* spiritual, friend *and* stranger, personal *and* communal.

The "old geezers" do struggle with the issues of today because many of them are still using religious practices, understandings, and theology that no longer fit the signs of our times. What are the questions or social issues that we must face today? Economic inequality, refugee crisis, immigrants, homelessness, protection of life in all forms. No wonder they feel so helpless and fearful! But the Church has a long history of facing new challenges, and of searching the Gospels and Tradition for answers and initiatives that will nourish and nurture the faith and lives of the people of God.

Chapter 3

DO I REALLY HAVE TO FORGIVE? YES, YOU DO!

AMONG THE MANY groups from whom I receive invitations to speak is a Catholic women's group in Ventura County that has been meeting regularly for more than twenty years. The members are mostly women with advanced educations, and many of them are involved in parish ministry. Listening to the stories, the expressed needs, the questions, and hearing the suggested topics of discussion from this and other similar groups, I have come to realize that an area ripe for exploration is that of forgiveness. It seems that many Catholics use traditional terms, both theological and biblical, without fully comprehending their full import and proper application to their lives. I think that forgiveness is one of these areas.

First, I want to ask the very real question, What *is* forgiveness? *Forgiveness* is a biblical word that means "to let go" in order to live in the present moment. It is an act of the will, a decision to let go of the desire to get even with someone who has hurt you in some way. From the Judeo-Christian perspective, it is a commandment from God, not a suggestion: This is about living in freedom as God's beloved children. It is vital to our inner peace and health. Forgiveness relieves us of our "stuckness" in the past to live more fully in the present. We forgive to get back into the flow of God's energy of love.

Just for a moment, stop reading. Sit quietly and take a deep breath. Hold it as long as you can, and feel the tightness, the tension, and the "stuckness" that grip your body. Then let the breath go and experience the flow of life once more. That is what the act of forgiveness can feel like in our spirit.

Forgiveness is primarily a gift that we give ourselves, and secondarily a gift we give to another person. While reconciliation is a gift we give to the community, and secondarily a gift we give to ourselves. Often we can confuse and magnify the struggle with the forgiveness process because we put the need for forgiveness, our hope for reconciliation, and desire for personal justice all in the same bucket. However, we need to differentiate among these three important aspects of right human relationships.

Forgiveness does not *approve* of the behavior or actions of the other. Rather, it recognizes that something has happened to upset, hurt, or affront us. We may even be scandalized by the words or actions of the perpetrator. Feelings of betrayal, disappointment, or violation may not disappear in this process, but we come to realize that we do not need to be entrapped by them. The process itself can inform us, enrich us, and mature us if we face the lessons of the painful encounter.

To choose not to forgive is like drinking poison and hoping the other person will die. How misguided and shortsighted we can be! Choosing not to forgive is to remain a perennial victim of those who have hurt us. They continue to abuse us through our own negative thoughts and feelings, setting up a "no win" situation, imprisoning us in a toxic emotional environment inside our heart. Forgiveness is the treatment of choice for anger and violence.

Forgiveness opens the door for the possibility of reconciliation, but it does not presume that it necessarily will conclude with reconciliation. Forgiveness gives us a new perspective on reality. The wounds are still present, but now they are transformed.

Reconciliation is then possible when the aggrieved seeks to renegotiate the relationship with a bit more insight and self-awareness. Admittedly, the relationship will almost certainly not be the same. Perhaps this is for the best, in that both individuals or groups have learned from the forgiveness process not to take each other for granted.

In the context of a discussion about forgiveness, it might be helpful to draw a distinction between *regret*, which requires no forgiveness, and *guilt*, which does. Regret, I think, is the emotional response to an event or action that caused unintentional hurt or harm, whereas guilt is the proper response when harm has been intended. Guilt generates the need for forgiveness while regret does not.

Justice is the righting of an imbalance or wrong—for example, the return of borrowed money or the public admission of a wrong. This is not always possible, but certainly desirable. Often this desire may need to be addressed in the reconciliation process as a separate component to rectifying the relationship.

What often complicates the task of forgiveness is that we all have different misconceptions about forgiveness. I would like to highlight several of these:

- **Forgiveness can be rushed.** Not so! Forgiveness can never be rushed; it takes time to heal, and to sift, through the ashes of what has happened to us in the wounding experience. It's like the experience of being burned, whether by sunburn, a hot iron, or even radiation treatment associated with cancer. Damage is done to the tissues that is not always visible and sometimes we don't even know how deeply that damage has penetrated. Only a clear, attentive, medicinal approach and the passage of time can bring the possibility of healing. And forgiveness is a part of that medicinal approach.

- **Forgiveness is a weakness.** Not so! During the U.S. civil rights upheaval of the 1960s, much violence was heaped upon innocent people. I remember the story of a white civil rights worker who, in the middle of one fracas, was pinned against a wall and mercilessly beaten for his interventions in the violence against people of color. One of the worker's friends saw the altercation and went to his aid, albeit too late. As he lifted him up from the ground, he questioned his friend's seemingly irrational determination to stand and not run or defend himself. His friend's response was classic and memorable: "The violence must stop somewhere. It stops here in my body. I will stand firm against this tide of violence and hatred."

- **To forgive is to forget.** Not so! We remember the pain of the incident so that we can avoid falling into a similar situation again in the future. Years ago, I lent a very good friend of mine a large sum of money with the promise of repayment within a few months. When I tried to contact him about six months later for repayment, there was no reply. It quickly became obvious to me that he did not intend to repay me. I was angry, hurt, and felt betrayed. Somehow, betrayal by friends cuts deep. As I worked through the process of forgiveness, I realized that I had been naive. I learned a very important lesson: We should never lend another person money unless we are willing to write it off as a gift or a loss.

- **Only large matters are issues for forgiveness.** Not so! We practice forgiving in small matters so that we can more easily handle the big stuff when it comes.

- **Forgiveness is easy.** Not so! Many years ago in my first parish, I made the acquaintance of Jack and Dorothy (not their real names). They had two small daughters, Catherine and Jessica. One day Catherine fell ill and was taken to the doctor's office. As the doctor checked the girl's eyes, he touched them with his unwashed fingers. Shortly thereafter, Catherine contracted an extremely debilitating disease that left her in a vegetative state. The negligence of the doctor was a verified fact. However, instead of following the path of litigation (which certainly would have been quite reasonable), the parents chose the process of forgiveness and acceptance of the painful new reality of their oldest daughter's life. Justice was not served, and this could have been a lingering wound in their psyche. However, Jack told me that they were able to transform their feelings of anger, resentment, and the desire to punish by focusing on the message of the cross of Christ: Father, forgive them for they know not what they have done! The power of this story has never left me, although thirty-five years have lapsed. And I ask myself: what would I have done?

- **One doesn't have to forgive if the other person doesn't deserve or want to be forgiven.** Not so! It's not about "the other"—it's about me. In this instance, I need to focus on my own end of the business. Besides, *deserve* is such a loaded word. Who judges who deserves what? As for the other not wanting forgiveness, I can't change what goes on in the mind and heart of others. I can, however, change what goes on in me.

God is forever forgiving us our trespasses. As Thomas Merton wisely observed, God is mercy within mercy. Why does God consistently do this? So that we might learn from our mistakes and grow and mature as human beings. What are we to forgive? Anything and anyone that prevents us from being authentically ourselves. Here is a short list to get you started:

- You and your own shortcomings
- Your parents and family for their inconsistences or shortcomings
- Betrayal by lover, spouse, partner
- Betrayal by friends or relatives
- Failure of children to live up to your expectations

- The failure to achieve hoped-for success in your career due to the action or omission of others
- Those who have gossiped about you or been mean to you
- Past hurts or grievances by individuals or groups
- Friends or people in general who have not met your expectations
- Violence in words or actions against you or your loved ones
- Institutions like the Church, corporations, the military-industrial complex, the government
- God, for not answering your prayers

It is very challenging and often quite difficult to enter the forgiveness process. It takes courage, self-understanding, and persistence to work through the many traps that we can fall into. Obstacles come in all shapes and sizes. Here are some of the many cul-de-sacs that we can find ourselves caught in:

- **Ongoing abuse.** This can take the form of domestic abuse, alcohol or drug addiction of a family member, frequent harassment at work, a neighbor's ongoing noise issues, parish conflicts, and so on.
- **Self-blame or inadequate sense of self.** This can be experienced as a default position when anything goes wrong (e.g., "It must have been my fault," "I deserve this treatment," "God is punishing me," "I don't deserve to be happy").

- **Self-sabotage.** Often this is rooted in a sub-conscious need to punish ourselves for some real or imagined transgression or omission. Self-sabotage can take many forms such as accidents, constant unexplained failures, or general emotional malaise.
- **Geographical separation.** The inner work of forgiveness does not depend on distance. It is about the presence and intention of the aggrieved, not the location of the perpetrator.
- **The person is dead.** Remember, forgiveness is about letting go of the toxic connection that you still have with the one who has hurt you. Forgiveness can reach beyond the grave.
- **The need to forgive God.** All relationships, including our relationship with God, need to be in harmony and integrity. Years ago, when I had finished my graduate studies at Fordham University in New York, I was packing up my belongings and sensed that the Lord was inviting me to mail my books back home without insurance or registration. Trusting that somehow or other that God had a different plan for me, I followed this "sense." It did not turn out the way I expected: I lost all my books in transit! On a conscious level, I thought I had let the loss go and moved on in my life; however, on another level, I had not. I was doing only light reading and nothing that would further my own growth in formation. One morning I sensed God saying to me, "You're angry at me." "Oh no, Lord," I said, "I'm not angry at you. Why

do you say that?" "You have not read anything of importance since you left Fordham." In a moment of embarrassing clarity, I realized that God was right. I was trying to punish God by not using my intellect in a wise and disciplined fashion. I asked God's forgiveness and then returned to my academic reading, rightfully chastened.

- **A moving or undefined target.** There is an enormous challenge when we need to forgive a corporate entity like church, government, society, or a particular group. Often there is no identifiable individual, and this can frustrate the process. Furthermore, the hurt may be multifaceted, running at a deeper level than we realize.

Forgiveness is an undertaking that must be embarked upon with a respectful attitude. It is the heroic journey, a task that can involve prayer, reflection, ritual expression, and deep emotional engagement. This process is about giving back something different or transformative to the one who has offended us. Fr. Ronald Rolheiser uses the metaphor of a water filter to describe this action. Whatever negativity we receive from the other, we are to transform or filter out this negativity and give back something positive. Therefore, like Jesus, we are to be filters, not lightning rods. This does not happen quickly. It takes time and honesty to face our painful emotions and transform them. As William Blake, the English poet said, "We go to hell for energy and to heaven for form, and learn to marry the two." We bring an embodied form to this demanding work when we engage ritual means of expressing our angst. This might mean burning a letter from some painful correspondence, burying a gift from a friend who has betrayed us, or giving away possessions from a former life situation. To live the symbolic life is to live the authentic religious life.

Our prayer and reflection propel us into deeper maturity through this process of forgiveness and transformative thinking. Here we see the kingdom of God at work. When we choose to forgive and do the demanding work of forgiveness, we are changed from the inside out. We create the possibility for greater happiness, freedom, and flourishing.

What about when we need to seek forgiveness from someone else? How do we apologize for our transaction? Dr. Gary Chapman and Jennifer Thomas have written an extremely helpful book entitled *Five Languages of Apology: How to Experience Healing in All Your Relationships*. The authors point out that often we fail to find the right way of communicating our regret for what has happened. Each person has his or her own language of apology. We listen, as aggrieved persons, to hear certain words in order to determine if the individual is truly contrite. Speaking the correct language is imperative because apologies connect to the feelings of being wronged or unloved. Which of these phrases or languages or combinations thereof, do you need to hear?

1. Expressing regret: I am sorry!
2. Accepting responsibility: I was wrong.
3. Making restitution: What can I do to make it right?
4. Genuinely repenting: I will try not to do that again.
5. Requesting forgiveness: Will you please forgive me?

Finally, what are the steps to forgiveness? Here is one way to work through the process:

1. **Admit the hurt.** Reflect and acknowledge how deeply you have been wounded. Do not rush the process! You know you are ready to move on when you say, "I am tired of hurting. I am ready to move on."

2. **Admit and work through the resentment.** Acknowledge your desire to retaliate without acting on it. Perhaps create a symbolic ritual to adequately express your feelings. This stage is usually the most difficult because you must face your own interior dark emotions. You come face-to-face with your shadow side. Sometimes writing in a journal or talking to a wise friend can help you process this mine-field of conflicted thoughts and feelings.

3. **Choose to forgive and bless the other person.** This is the step where you actually say aloud, "I choose to forgive so and so for doing such and such to me. I ask God to bless them." Many people find it helpful to express this step in the form of a prayer in spoken or written form. This prayer is not about asking God to change the other person. This is the stage of letting go into God's hands the outcome of the other person's life.

4. **Seek to be reconciled as the Spirit leads you.** This stage is optional, in that now you just wait and see what presents itself. Does the offender contact you? Do you coincidentally run into

your coworker in the grocery store? Do you receive an unsolicited phone call? These could all be signs that God is inviting you to step into the reconciliation process.

I don't know what struggles the women of Ventura County have in forgiving those who have hurt them; but I'm sure, like all good, decent human beings, they have a deep desire to understand the process of forgiveness and to go about the hard work of bringing this crucial human action into their lives, the lives of their family, their faith group, their community, and their nation.

Chapter 4

BEYOND THE USUAL BOUNDARIES

NESTLED IN THE foothills of Los Padres National Forest is the beautiful seaside city of Santa Barbara. This colorful Southern California community is a wealthy enclave that annually embraces thousands of tourists and visitors. Its elegant main street is lined with attractive shops and boutique restaurants, an environment enhanced by Spanish architecture and exquisite landscaping. The visitor is embraced by a riot of color and beauty. On a hill overlooking the city, Mission Santa Barbara is a reminder to the citizens of the intersection of faith and society, and of the city's Franciscan foundation.

Many years ago, I was invited to speak to the Word and Life Study Fellowship, a group of thoughtful Christians in search of a mature faith that has met weekly for over forty years at a local church premises. The group has outgrown its original home in the Catholic Church complex and moved elsewhere. Members of the group come from varied backgrounds, careers, and life experiences, bringing with them challenging and penetrating questions.

In its early years, the group studied the Bible with great interest and enthusiasm, but at the conclusion of the Bible Study (after twenty-one years), they decided to make their choices more eclectic, seeking books dealing directly or indirectly with the interface between faith and society. One of the many attractions of this group is its function as a community of believers sharing a mutual hunger for intellectual nourishment in relation to faith. They are not afraid to address the tough questions of life. I have been privileged to meet with them about twice a year. Each year they choose two different books for study and discussion. The invited presenter is asked to share his or her insights, focused on a chapter in the book. The presentation is followed by questions, discussion of the material, and a shared experience of prayer.

While this is not a specifically Catholic group, it embraces the best principles of active and critical discussion of, and reflection on, the increasingly complex business of living a fully human life, which is lived in the light of faith and reason, justice and compassion. In other words, the "and" factor—both this and that.

Catholicism at its best is a balanced religion in that it embraces this reality: for example, the material and the spiritual, the active and the contemplative, the recognition of the need for both worship and service. This dynamic allows for a synergistic energy that is translated into a more comprehensive expression of our humanity and hence, our faith. Faith is pointless and dangerous if it is not grounded in the reality of present circumstances. There is no such thing as a private faith. Faith by its very definition is a personal response expressed in the public arena through my value system. The personal and the public come together in the communal space. The choices we make are based on this value system, which is continuing to be formed by our personality, family, culture, life experience, education, and sense of Mystery or the Divine. What do you believe in? What is your value system? How do you make your own decisions?

Many people turn to religion for help in answering some of the big questions of life. Others turn to science. Some look to individual mentors, while others rely on their own inner sense of guidance. For many years, religion and science did not cohabit well in people's minds. Today we recognize that the revelation of truth can be either revealed or discovered. Truth is truth, whether it is a scientific truth or a religious truth. Our understanding of truth, and its application, determines the locus of authority. Is it something that you can live with because you fully "believe" it, that is, it comes from inside you, or is it something you accept because someone with a title or an office has told you so (e.g., doctor, reverend, pope, or president)?

Our understanding of ourselves (psychology) will have a significant—if unconscious—impact on our belief in God (theology). Study and reflection on this relationship will then affect our perception of, and interaction with, other people (sociology). How we understand and relate to human beings (anthropology) in general will then influence the way we read the Scriptures, perceive reality, and relate to the Cosmos (cosmology). Studies of the subatomic world (quantum physics and mechanics) are being matched by the mysteries of the multiple universes in the cosmos (astrophysics and astronomy). We live in exciting times, in which we are invited to ask deeper and more meaningful questions to help us make better connections. These are the type of new and stimulating books that Word and Life enjoy reading and studying—books that interface with different fields of study, a variety of voices, life experiences, and contemporary issues. Eleanor Roosevelt once famously said, "Small people talk about other people, average people talk about events, great people talk about ideas." The sharing of ideas in a courteous and civil discussion is an art essential to human maturing.

Each of us, in our own way and through our own life experience, is invited on an incredible journey of ongoing conversion—letting go of outdated judgments and belief systems that no longer fit our reality. This is difficult but necessary work in the process of becoming fully human. One of the methods that can help us in this quest is an ancient practice of examining and analyzing our thoughts. John Cassian, a wise and honored monk of the fourth century, invites the serious believer to follow a three-step process in doing this reflective work:

1. Notice the thought for what it is—a thought.
2. Choose to replace the thought with something more positive—a Scripture passage, a pleasant memory, or a beautiful image.
3. Focus on what you are grateful for—perhaps you can make a short list.

Monitoring our thoughts is a mature religious discipline that helps us to make better connections and improve our relationships.

Many religious people have divorced their practice of regular worship from the equal and necessary practice of service to others. Both nourish each other and ideally flow out into the world, making it a better place. In theology, we call this discovering God in the transcendent experience (worship) and the immanent reality (service). Both awaken us and connect us to the ever-present Creator who is in all things and yet beyond all things.

Every age and culture faces its own challenges and short-comings in its yearning for human maturity. This is especially true when we talk about spiritual maturity. North America has been blessed in so many ways that it is easy to overlook its societal shortcomings. However, while we are proud of and grateful for our accomplishments, and the moral leadership that we have heretofore provided the world, it is necessary to name and honestly face some of our inadequacies in order to continue to grow in maturity and compassion. In our culture, it seems that the following themes threaten to undercut the apparent blessings:

1. Materialism
2. Individualism
3. A sense of restlessness
4. Gun violence
5. Exceptionalism
6. Inequality of wealth
7. Racism
9. Failure to address climate change
10. Lack of eco-friendly use of the resources of the earth

In my experience, most of these themes are regularly avoided in religious circles. They might receive a mention in a written document or two, or might even be talked about in a homily, but rarely are they honestly addressed in our families and communities. These are the very topics that the prophets of old, and today, speak about with such great fervor. They are the measure of our true religious instinct and spiritual practice.

I readily confess that I find these themes to be personally challenging. Often we put our focus on the areas that require less energy, or that do not force us to admit our own prejudices or biases. Or we can slip into comparisons with others. This is why conversion and transformation are always at the heart of any real change. Gifts and blessings are meant to be shared with others, not just our family, or friends, or socioeconomic peers. The responsibility of our blessings is to move us to actively respond to the needs around us, to remind us that we are all connected. We are indeed our brother's keeper (Gen 4:9–10).

Groups such as Word and Life, who are courageous enough to enter into conversations about these challenging topics, set an example that invites us to read, study, reflect, and act in new ways that are liberating and transformative for ourselves and others. To broaden our minds, expand our understanding, and ponder on the meaning of the interconnectedness of humanity, the planet, and the cosmos.

Chapter 5

TWELVE-STEP GROUP

Getting to the Heart of Things

IN 1992, I was sent to Fordham University in New York for further studies in preparation for my new role as a consultant in adult religious education. During this time, I was a resident at Christ the King Parish in the South Bronx. For all the people of this area, life was both tough and dangerous. The Church was a beacon of hope and stability for the deeply wounded and emotionally crippled, and for those clinging to their faith in an unfriendly world. One of the ways the parish provided hope and support was by offering the church basement for use by the local Alcoholics Anonymous group, which met every Tuesday evening. I was privileged to be a regular part of the group as an observer, through an agreement between the group and my director of studies. In the process, I was able to begin to face my own demons of overwork and codependency. The stories were incredibly painful to hear, as tears and laughter greeted the outpouring of human anguish, hope, and survival. As I witnessed this group being authentically present to each other, I couldn't help but reflect upon the many theological words that we use, but often misunderstand, in the context of the complexity, and what Pope Francis calls the "messiness," of human life. Here was the Church at its best. As Francis has said repeatedly, the Church must be like a field hospital attending to the wounded of the world.

All human beings are created in God's image, but what does that really mean? How can that be real in our lives, especially when we go through such painful circumstances? This basic, but important, truth reminds us that the seed of divinity is embedded within us. Julian of Norwich once said, "Now the seed of a hazelnut tree grows into a hazelnut tree, the seed of a pear tree grows into a pear tree, and the seed of God grows into God." As bearers of the seeds of God, we grow into our full humanity through the unfolding of our life, with all its tragedies and triumphs. The familial term that we use for this intimate metaphor is *children*. We are God's children, all of us, sinners and saints, scoundrels and elite, rich and poor alike. To experience this love of God is pure grace. We have not earned it; it is complete gift. God loves us not because we are good but because God is good.

We learn this love in a community of persons. This is why creating and building community is so important to Christianity. One of the hallmark teachings of Jesus is that we are to discover his presence in relationships and gatherings: "For where two or three are gathered together in my name, there am I in the midst of them" (Matt 18:20). Inclusivity is one of the signs of a truly Christian community, where all are welcome. I remember one day, at an open twelve-step meeting, three separate people stood up and thanked the group for being present for them: "Without you, I would be dead now." How many people do not feel welcome in our Church communities, are turned away or rejected for one reason or another?

How many are dead, literally or symbolically, because we have failed to do what Jesus did—invite them in out of the cold? Remember Jesus personally invited Judas Iscariot and Peter, two men who would betray him.

God sees us as already whole and complete. It is up to us to participate in this work of completion. As Christians, we describe this as "growing in the likeness of Jesus, our model of true humanity." We gradually strip away the inconsistencies, the untruths, and the undue attachments to discover our true nature. This effort is called conversion. It is a slow but steady work of seeing and experiencing our life from a new perspective. Such transformative labor is rewarded with a sense of peace or humble acceptance of life as it is. Albert Nolan, OP, in his classic book *Jesus Before Christianity*, gives us a surprising and dramatic perspective on this: "Jesus discovered his divinity in the transcendent depths of his humanity." And so it is with us! God will do God's part, but we must do our own part in working through our struggles, not alone but in tandem with others, guided by God's great love for us.

This is why twelve-step groups work for so many people—because participants admit their need for a Higher Power as they face their own shortcomings and seek reconciliation with and among others. As one sober man in recovery said, "We alcoholics are misguided mystics!" He is right. Addicts and alcoholics need to be guided in the process of being reconciled with their identity. Reconciliation is the labor of making peace with the past to move forward. It is the effort of finding ways to be in right relationship with others. This is the core work of holiness—becoming fully human. Reconciliation is normally prefaced by the practice of forgiveness, beginning with oneself. Forgiveness involves the emotional process of letting go of blame to focus on living in peace and harmony with all parts of ourselves.

These alcoholics and addicts from all walks of life and social backgrounds may not have studied theology, but they are certainly actively struggling to live out the great truths that a healthy theology offers. No one needs to tell them about hell and damnation, because they have suffered through it. Their days and nights of loneliness, self-condemnation, self-loathing, and self-inflicted pain have made it clear that this is not living as a child of God. In their recovery process, they are now seeking fulfillment in a completely new way: they are experiencing salvation—the path of healing and wholeness.

Let me give you an example of this collaborative process through this unusual but true story of a porn addict. Years ago, I knew of a man who struggled with a powerful addiction to pornography that had come to rule his life. He had made promises and bargains with God along the way, but finally, in despair, one night he somehow decided to honestly face the core of his addiction. He lined up five of his favorite pictures, placed them before his chair, and sat down. "God," he said, "I am not leaving here until you reveal to me the real reason why I am so drawn to these pictures. What is it that has me so captivated by these naked bodies?" For over an hour, he sat in that chair with no clear revelation. The he removed two of the photos and continued his vigil. An hour passed with no further insight. Then he removed two more photos. Now he sat with the one remaining photo that he had possessed since he was nineteen. Again, he repeated his desperate prayer: "I am not leaving here until you reveal to me what's behind this entrapment." The man sat there for forty-five more minutes and then in one painful moment, the revelation came, and in his words,

"The addiction broke open." There is meaning hidden within everything, including our brokenness.

Theologically we are fond of the terms *redemption* and *salvation*, but do we know what they really mean? In this setting in the South Bronx, I came to think more deeply about these somewhat technical words. Redemption is the historical fact of Christ's total giving of himself ("sacrifice") for and with all people, while salvation is our acceptance and application of this gift to our own life. Redemption is a onetime event. Salvation is a continuing, daily embracing of the trust that we are inherently good, loved, and accepted. No one can do this for us! Others can stand in solidarity with us, but we must do it for ourselves. In this light, twelve-step groups work for many people because in them people are given clear daily steps in the salvific process. They learn to practice these steps regularly in relation to their Higher Power.

Confronting temptations is a regular and necessary part of this process. Just as Jesus confronted his primary struggle and dark voices of temptation (Luke 4:1–13), so must we. This story offers us a great metaphor of a battle with evil, and it is indeed a battle, for our authentic humanity. Jesus's temptations revolved around the use of his power, prestige, and possessions. What are your core temptations? Did you happen to notice in this story that it was the Spirit that sent him into the desert for this encounter? Because this inner work was an essential initiation into his life's ministry. Did you also pay attention to the fact that these temptations would return? So it is with us. Our life's temptations to be less than our authentic self will return often, with a variety of faces and circumstances. This is one of the great gifts of twelve-step spirituality, to help us face our core temptations so that we can uncover the gold inside.

Some Christians use the term *born again* to describe this new acceptance of one's obvious shortcomings or need for change. They are referencing the passage in John 3:3–8 where Jesus is speaking with the Pharisee Nicodemus about the new life that comes with conversion. *Born again* is a metaphor for experiencing God and ourselves in a new way. Often this happens after a transformative experience such as a trauma or ecstasy or, more commonly, a major life decision to turn in a different direction. Recovering alcoholics do not usually use this term in reference to their radical change. Instead, they will say things like, "I thank God for my alcoholism because it woke me up," or, "It saved me from myself." Such dramatic, poetic language instinctually speaks to those people who have felt like wretches separated from God's amazing grace of undeserving love.

One of the signs of authentic conversion or "waking up" according to twelve-step spirituality is service to others, especially those others who need to wake up to their own addictions. This generativity is grounded in the real lived experience of someone who has fallen and has discovered how to get up. Their work of service comes from their authentic identity and not from their ego. It makes for a genuine encounter with the other, which in turn encourages the other person to conversion.

Flowing from this line of thinking, morality is then seen not as an external list of good things to do to get to heaven, but as a way of being in the world—a way of right relationship. It is living in congruity with truth, beauty, goodness, and all living beings. We all seek this fulfillment in one way or another. In this light, temptation is the enticement not to live up to one's authentic self, one's call to fulfillment. Heaven and hell are states of being, rather than places per se. They represent metaphors of being in right relationship (holiness) or living in isolation from one's true self (torment). It is only love that bridges the great divide and brings union. St. Catherine of Siena said it this way, "It is heaven all the way to heaven and hell all the way to hell." May we journey together in a heavenly procession!

The Cathedral of Our Lady of the Angels in Los Angeles images this procession in a unique and heart-lifting way. Along the walls of the main space, leading to the sanctuary, hang a series of breathtakingly beautiful tapestries depicting the procession of the saints—of all of us—toward our heavenly home. The artist, John Nava, has portrayed people of all cultures, ages, demeanors, and eras—people from Europe, Africa, the Americas, Asia, from the earliest days of Christianity through the Dark Ages, the Middle Ages, the Renaissance, and the centuries following. However, it is the faces of people of the South Bronx thirty years ago that I see most vividly, and I know that they are gathered up in that procession as well. I note, too, that in his wisdom, Nava has left several saints unnamed. They represent you and me, making our way home toward God in the company of those who have gone before us and those who walk with us in faith in friendship, in twelve-step programs, and in community, wherever we find it.

Chapter 6

AFTER ALL THESE YEARS, WHERE ARE WE?

ON THE EASTERN edge of Melbourne, Australia, the middle-class suburb of Wheelers Hill lies in the foothills of the Dandenong Ranges. The area was settled in the sixties and seventies, when orchards and market gardens gave way to suburban development. Young couples just starting their families moved in. Among these were a group of women whom I have come to know and interact with for over twenty years in their spiritual searching. The Bethany group, as they call themselves, consists of mostly professional women who have had a strong bond of friendship for over fifty years. They participated in the building of the local Catholic parish and belonged to a vibrant parish community for many years. They are cradle Catholics who have been regularly meeting in each other's homes over the years for support and encouragement in their lives. They are teachers, nurses, an accountant, pastoral minister, a scientist, and homemakers. They are married or widowed with grown children and grandchildren, most of whom have left the Church. They dare to ask the tough, challenging questions that every adult believer must ask if they are to mature in their faith.

These women are no longer comfortable with many of the simplistic, black-and-white truths they grew up with because they do not fit the context of their lives or their family or work relationships. All kinds of moral, ethical, and sexual questions have arisen with their children and grandchildren, which demand new and more nuanced responses. Like many of their peers, they are seeking meaning in the ordinary details of their lives: family, career, community, Church, and political life. They want to move away from ingrained religious habit and adolescent rebellion, to intelligent interaction with the issues at hand. In a word, they are seeking a realistic adult spirituality, springing from an informed conscience, that can nurture and sustain them at this time in their human questing. Unfortunately, these women feel like believers in exile because many of the ordained leaders of the Church do not want to realistically engage them and their questions. In addition, the cultural and ecclesial environment in Australia—including recent developments in social media and information access, the almost complete absence of religion from public discourse and decision-making, the ongoing devastating effects of the clergy abuse scandal, and the importation of foreign-born clergy who often have different cultural values, a heightened sense of clerical status, and patriarchal expectations—challenges the certainties of religious identification.

In fact, as we know, the Church is a world of believers with a plethora of different stories, highly diverse psychological backgrounds, emotional makeups, spiritual inclinations, and cultural mores. One of my favorite images of Church is that of a great umbrella. It gathers us together around the one story of Jesus Christ and protects us from the inclement weather of nihilism, meaninglessness, and loneliness. The Church does not always live up to our expectations—whether in administration, clerical behavior, political correctness, pastoral responses, and, most significantly, the inclusion of women as full participants. This was most poignantly summarized by the American Jesuit Walter Burghardt, speaking in 1973 at the baptism of a child:

> Sonia Maria, before we welcome you through symbol and ritual into this paradoxical people, this community of contradictions, let me make an uncommonly honest confession. In the course of half a century (and more), I have seen more Catholic corruption than most Catholics read of. I have tasted it; I have been reasonably corrupt myself. And yet I joy in this Church, this living, sinning people of God. I love it with a crucifying passion. Why? For all the Catholic hate, I experience here a community of love. For all the institutional idiocy, I find here a tradition of reason. In the midst of death, I hear here an incomparable stress on life. For all the apparent absence of God, I sense here the presence of Christ. I pray Sonia Maria, that your life within this community, your experience of a strange god and still stranger people, will rival mine. (Piper and Doherty, *The Attachment*, 208)

In fact, as Burghardt implies, realistically, the best that the Church can do is point us in the direction of God. Tonight, the Bethany group discussion is to be based on Sr. Joan Chittister's book *Faith and Belief*. Sylvia begins with the question, "Why do we all remain Catholic, given the way things are?" The conversation centers around the themes of community support, familiarity with the religious tribal identity, cultural influence, birth into this specific religious consciousness, nurturance, and sacramental experience.

The Canadian Jesuit Bernard Lonergan has said that all human beings are born with an insistent drive to ask questions, to know, and to understand. As I see it, the beginning of an adult faith is evidenced in the intelligent questioning of religious authority and of the official teachings of the Church, just as an adolescent questions parental authority to discover his or her own inner authority and value system. The effort to truly experience and interpret the Divine Mystery in our own life is a lonely struggle because the journey requires that we encounter doubt and confusion along the way. French philosopher and writer Voltaire frames this work: "Doubt is an uncomfortable position, but certainty is a ridiculous one!" Doubt reflects my own limitations and uncertainties. Strangely enough, doubt is the sibling of faith; the two work together in symmetry to create a broader-based approach to religion. I see the Bethany group doing this work together, and I suspect that this is an instinctive way for women to engage in this vital search for meaning.

Good religion is about understanding *and* experience, and it accommodates doubt. All three have their place in the stories of salvation (liberation), in both the Jewish and Christian Scriptures. Keep in mind that certainty is not a feature of, nor a prerequisite for, holiness. Witness the many stories of the saints and their eclectic journeys toward wholeness. Too few of us wrestle with the God who has been presented to us in childhood. We either accept God's existence as a given because that's the tradition we've received, or we've inherited a disbelief in God's existence, generally from family, teachers, or community (Gerard Windsor, *The Tempest Tossed Church*, 91).

What about superstition? Is it true that all religions accommodate some forms of superstition, as atheists often claim? Superstition is the opposite of faith; it is about control. It is simply the desire to shortcut a real encounter with the Divine. Whether it is through a particular sign, symbol, story, prayer form, or activity, superstition promises results. God will be persuaded, or coerced, or shamed, into responding to our efforts. Faith, however, is a relationship with God with no guarantees; it is about trust. Ideally, faith is nurtured within community, as the Bethany group attests.

Superstition grows out of our own fears and insecurities and shortchanges our need for an adult relationship with God. In this context, Thomas Merton once said the biggest temptation is to settle for too little. So it is for many Christian believers. The Christian inheritance is essentially a story that has spawned a multitude of connected stories, which implies various necessary interpretive renditions of those stories. The real question is this: Does your interpretation of *the* story as it intersects with the story of your life set you free or liberate you into the fullness of your humanity? If not, then you have not encountered the Creator who is forever creating and re-creating reality. God, or Ultimate Mystery, is Transcendent, Incarnate, and Immanent, which means that the Creator is embedded in creation and yet beyond it at the same time. God is a communion of relationships that is experienced in our vibrant encounters with reality. When we experience communion with another person, with creation, music, art, or our life work, we experience some aspect of God's presence in our midst. The essential tension in Christianity is between the transcendent (the world of unseen things) and the incarnational (the historical and empirical reality). Is this not like the tension that parents face in raising their children: living in the present reality with an eye toward the future? The complexities of life are an opportunity for us to see and experience God's invitation to enter our life as a partner. The other side of this amazing equation is that God invites us to enter God's life as partners. Our responsibility in this relationship is to *allow* God to work in us and through us. This is what is called the ever-expanding task of love.

Several members of Bethany group have shared how they have lost their faith. Australian author Gerard Windsor offers this insight: People often "lose religion" because it becomes less and less a part of their atmosphere or their family. People think themselves out of religion rather than into it. We tend to focus on our shortcomings and ourselves rather than the gaze of God's love, as Jesus did (Windsor, 118).

Quite understandably, loss of faith or abandonment of religion is often caused by an unexplainable trauma in our life, the loss of a loved one, unanswered prayers, the loss of a "voice" in community, frustration at a priest or person of authority in the Church, or anger at the Church for some specific grievance. This is not uncommon, as the loss of faith signals a loss of a previous level of faith or maturity that we have outgrown. Authentic faith is always growing and developing. What worked when we were young does not necessarily help us when we are older because the context of our life has changed so much. Faith is like a living tree that grows upward and downward, deepening us and broadening us.

When my nephew Matthew was twelve, he was diagnosed with Crohn's disease. Now Matthew was one of those adorable kids that every mother yearns for: intelligent, outgoing, friendly, athletic, and good looking. How could such a devastating disease afflict such a good boy? Where was God in all this? I asked Matthew how he was dealing with his own suffering. His response surprised me: "I look at Uncle Dave and how he has dealt with his paralysis and it gives me courage to face my own struggle. I also talk to God a lot." Such simple and trusting faith in the unknown. When I questioned his father (my brother), about how he was doing with his son's condition, Tony was understandably angry and anxious about Matthew's future. He said, "I no longer believe what I believed before." "Is it possible," I queried, "that you are being invited to shed your old way of seeing God for a more expansive approach?" "What do you mean?" he shot back. "I mean that God is inviting you to make room for your deep feelings of anxiety, fear, impotent frustration, and sense of divine betrayal. Your old image of God no longer exists. God is offering you a new expanded image." This did not immediately console him, as you might understand. This would involve some real work on his part, a shift in his role in "working with God." I can share with you that Tony has embraced this lesson and grown tremendously in his relationship with God and takes his spiritual path seriously. His mature perception of the Divine is a credit to his disciplined spiritual practice. That transition is not easy for most people and seemingly impossible for many. What kind of connection with God or with Jesus is possible in light of the great struggles of our lives? Most of us grew up with an image of Jesus as a kind of "Teflon" man with only a surface likeness to us. Once the temptations in the desert were dealt with, he could proceed along the path of perfection. He didn't have to struggle to develop his own adult faith. But the Scriptures tell a different story. The desert temptation stories are only a fleeting image of a lifelong adult quest.

Gerard Windsor offers an interesting perspective on the adult Jesus. He discerns three characteristics of Jesus outlined in the Gospels that need to be named:

1. his autonomy: he discovered power within himself;
2. his strangely remote, enigmatic, and sometimes
   antisocial means of social interaction; and
3 his capacity to reveal a world beyond our natural mundane experiences (79).

Life for him was not a bed of roses. Nevertheless, to his last
breath he remained faithful to the quest. As for him, so for us. So
where does this leave us? *Be faithful to the person that God has
created you to be.* For some of us, this means falling in love with
Jesus. But for most, it's an intellectual commitment to loving
others as you yourself want to be loved. This perspective reflects
our personality differences. One size does not fit everyone. The
pattern of our living is toward self-transcendence—to grow, to
push beyond our basic nature, experiencing intimations of the
Divine. This is what Jesus did and so it is for us. We get glimpses
of our divinity, or sanctified nature (Heb 10:10) in our best
moments or experiences of being human.

God is perfect; we are in a *process* of being perfected by
life and by grace. God sees us as already perfected in God's
gracious love. We are to trust God's perception of us, to see
ourselves as God sees us. To receive this gaze of God's love is
the necessary discipline of a believer. Otherwise we will attach
ourselves to any number of lesser visages. Jesus took on our
humanity (enfleshment) to affirm our basic goodness and to
affirm our embodiment, but most Christians have not received
this liberating message.

The essentials of the Christian faith are summarized in
our various creeds; these, however, are written in ecclesial,
theological language, difficult to grasp in its true meaning
by most people. What adds to the confusion is that there are
various layers of importance to these value statements. It is

the same in the Scriptures as well as in any catechism: not all statements are equally important or significant. Theologians and scripture scholars are constantly at work to help us to discern and focus on what really matters.

In our rationalist age, we are confronted with new challenges to faith: atheism, agnosticism, and scientism. In bygone days, these responses might have been lumped together under the one category of apostasy: a complete and utter rejection of religious faith.

One response that appeals to me deeply is that of well-known Australian priest and author Msgr. Tony Doherty, who has articulated his own credo of seven principles, one that he continues to develop and nuance over time:

1. Life, for all its mystery, has meaning.
2. Christ never tired of saying, "Do not be afraid."
3. The world is good.
4. Everything we search for is within us.
5. Unconditional forgiveness is what a prodigal God will always give us.
6. Love is the one important thing.
7. Our life is held in the gentle embrace of a gracious mystery whom Jesus calls the Father (Windsor, 181).

This man's credo is a result of a lifetime of study, prayer, reflection, and action. The women of Bethany group are involved in a similar search to articulate their adult faith. Sylvia's question was not answered that night, but I want to tell them that their daily lives of faithfulness, doubt, and striving for truth are Catholicism at its best.

Chapter 7
MEN'S WORK

Reconnecting with a Healthy Masculinity

SINCE THE 1990S, I have had the privilege of researching and studying in the field of men's psychology and spirituality. This has led me to offer retreats and workshops for men of widely varying ages and cultures throughout North America and beyond. Among the many events I have led, three widely geographically separated groups remain in my memory: these men were blue-collar workers, white-collar professionals, retired men, with some church workers, teachers, and even a few priests.

Their questions were eerily similar and their life experiences, although embedded in three distinct cultures (Newcastle, United Kingdom; Ottawa, Canada; and Southern California, United States), followed the same patterns. I also realized that their questions had been mine many years ago. What I have discovered and learned on my own journey has been both exciting and challenging. I have gained a deeper understanding of my own and others' humanity and the causes of my own struggles with coming to maturity. I have also learned ways to heal and nourish myself in order to enjoy my life more.

Here are some of the questions that kept recurring in these three retreat experiences:

- Questions of life—What's it all for?
- How do I nurture my own soul? (Prayer is not always enough.)
- What's the difference between religion and spirituality?
- How do I develop a healthy image of God?
- How do I deal with my own existential loneliness? (Reconnecting with the interior life)
- How do I understand the unnamed yearnings and desires of my heart?

So, indeed, what *is* it all for? Life is, in the proverbial sense, a search for meaning and deep connection with all that is. Most of us men are painfully disconnected from our interior life. We spend a great proportion of our life intersecting with the outer world of responsibility and activity and neglect the inner world of reflection and silence. This often leads to an impoverished or outdated image of God that is more likely a reflection of our own self-image, which might be judgmental, overly critical, or even inadequate in dealing with the trials and tribulations of daily life. From this impeded growth, many men then lead lives of quiet desperation, feeling alone and insecure, using their discretionary time to focus on nonessential interests (sports, cars, computers, or TV) rather than meaningful engagement with the interior life—until it is too late. Life gradually becomes filled with distractions, rather than with deeply meaningful relationships or encounters with the Divine.

And how to nurture my soul as a man? Let me address this question from a personal perspective. In 1995, I was introduced to M.A.L.E.S (Men As Learners and ElderS) through my work with Fr. Richard Rohr. This group, later renamed Illuman, continues to be a life-giving vehicle for men's transformation. It is an international movement dedicated to the transformation of men by men and has been enormously helpful to participants in grappling with issues of men's spirituality and our authentic service to the world.

Richard Holloway, in his book *Between the Monster and the Saint*, offers a challenging conclusion:

> It is a harsh world, indescribably cruel. It is a gentle world, unbelievably beautiful. It is a world that can make us bitter, hateful, rabid, destroyers of joy. It is a world that can draw forth tenderness from us, as we lean towards one another over broken gates. It is a world of monsters and saints, a mutilated world, but it is the only one we have been given. We should let it shock us not into hatred or anxiety, but into unconditional love.

My connection with Illuman helps me to love the world in concrete ways with an unconditional love, through the ongoing journey of understanding myself, others, and the ways in which we come to wholeness. There are practical tools to help us in this quest. Some of the best of these are centering prayer, rituals, stories, connection with nature, council work of sharing, grief work, and shadow work, as well as rites of passage designed to mark stages in the human journey undertaken by every man. These are best done in a supportive group.

Traditionally this can take the direction of making a retreat, which is a significant period dedicated to connecting with the Creator. This practice taps into the ancient Jewish practice of keeping the Sabbath as a day of rest and renewal.

Normally this time is given to prayer, worship, leisure activities, and renewal of relationships, all at a slower pace. In the Catholic perspective, this is why we keep Sundays as a day dedicated to this same value system. We have also added observances such as holy days of obligation, daily holy hours, days of recollection, retreats, and the like—to awaken us to the interior life.

Men's spirituality is a value system that flows from a relationship to a Higher Power. It is all about transformation; it pivots around what we call a man's "primal wound." This might be abandonment (by one's father), rejection (by one's mother), loss (of a significant other), betrayal (by a friend), internalized shame (from an inadequate sense of self). Real spirituality addresses these wounds in an honest, straightforward manner. This is the authentic work and meaning of salvation: helping us to grow in wholeness. Ideally, in the life of a man, power and authority go together—the inner and the outer. If these are not in right relationship, then we will tend to "worship" the outer power and authority, to the denigration of our own power and inner authority, with potentially terrifying results. James Hollis, in his wonderfully insightful book *Under Saturn's Shadow: The Wounding and Healing of Men*, describes this dynamic. As a psychoanalyst, he invites men to go deeper into their story to discover the significance behind their own yearnings for meaning and authentic expression.

A man's purpose in life is to use his power and authority in service to others; otherwise, interiorly he remains an adolescent caught in a self-centered approach to reality. This is where religion has a key role. Healthy religion acts as a powerful container into which the contents of a man's spirituality can be directed and guided to an appropriate and meaningful expression for the good of society. Religion, at its best, provides a cohesive language of the soul and offers a framework of spiritual practices through which a man can chart his journey into his full humanity. Many men do not understand this language; it is not readily familiar to us because it does not exist in the world of, for example, commerce, competition, the military, or politics. Rather, it serves the aspect of our humanity that is connected to our relationship with the Divine, with others, and with our deepest self.

In traditional language, this is called living the virtuous life. This entails the courageous effort to face our vices and uncover their deeper significance in our lives. We all have vices; they are the companions of our innate virtues. They work together to hone our virtues into something authentic and lasting. Every virtue has two vices working simultaneously, like a grinding stone to create a beautiful diamond out of the rough-cut stone of our life. For example, humility is considered by many one of the most important virtues for spiritual growth. On either side of humility, there is a vice to keep us balanced in the middle, for virtue (truth) is always in the middle. In this case, it is pride or hubris on one side and self-abnegation or false humility on the other. Both are enemies of the true self and must be tackled.

Here are some examples of tried and true ways that men can connect with this "soul" that animates, nourishes, and gives us courage to live our lives to the fullest, with authenticity:

- Connecting with nature (e.g., walking, hiking, even sitting quietly on a beach)
- Connecting with the animal world in the domestic scene or in the wild
- Prayer/meditation

- Artwork/poetry/music
- Healing of memories by revisiting the past (best done with professional support)
- Ritual and ceremony
- Body work (massage therapy, yoga, deep breathing, Tai Chi)
- Dream work and Active Imagination, which involve the interpretation and application of the meaning of dreams to daily life (we know from the biblical tradition that God speaks to us through dreams)
- Connection with mentors
- Risking deepening relationships and sharing feelings with others
- Finding a way of serving others
- Contemplation/centering prayer
- Journaling (write down your hopes and dreams, your thoughts and feelings)
- Recognizing that sometimes life sucks! We all have bad days, weeks, and months, even years.
- Experimenting with beginning your sentences with, "I'm angry that..."; "I'm sad that..."; "I hate that..."
- Telling stories, explore the great myths of the Bible and of literature
- Practicing forgiveness whenever you can
- Rediscovering playfulness

Another traditional way of nourishing a man's soul is through the liturgical rite of the Eucharist. As Catholic boys, we talked about "going to Mass" on Sunday. This was probably a good first step in understanding this potent mystery. However, it does not speak to the more complicated life of an adult male, especially if the celebration is not vibrant or engaging. Here is another way of understanding and applying this practice to our life: It is about becoming Eucharist for others. Let me explain. We are to *become* that which we celebrate. In the Eucharist, there are specific actions that we are to experience and then to emulate. Here is a summary of these actions:

Gathering Rite
- Gathering
- Welcoming
- Forgiving and being forgiven
- Praising
- Praying

Word
- Listening
- Reflecting
- Responding
- Interceding

Sacrament
- Receiving
- Offering up
- Blessing
- Breaking open
- Sharing
- Presence

Missioning Rite
- Sending forth
- Witnessing
- Serving

Liturgy is not so much what *we* do, but what *God* does through us. This helps us to face the mystery of our lives with courage and compassion, for we are not alone in this effort. A lecturer from whom I learned a great deal at Boston College, Rev. Michael Himes, was fond of saying, "That which is true always and everywhere must be noted, honored, and celebrated somewhere, somehow." These genuine actions are repeated for us so that *we* might *become* the actions in our relationships with others. To authentically become a eucharistic person means to regularly and mindfully practice these above actions in our daily lives.

Regarding a man's image of God, the first question to ask is from where does your image of God derive? Almost always from parents, religious authorities, and Scripture. There may be nothing wrong with these images, but they are rarely adequate to the complexities of adult development unless they are informed and deepened by a man's life experience. As life's challenges increase, a man needs to broaden his thinking to embrace images from his life experience—connection with nature and the outdoors, loving and faithful relationships, and the cosmos.

Because we have forgotten the great stories and myths of male development, we tend to forget that all of this has happened before; there is nothing new under the sun! This kind of forgetting can lead us to living our lives as victims or nursing our wounds interminably. Richard Rohr, OFM, has frequently shared his insight that if we do not transform our wounds, we will transmit them—to family, to friends, to colleagues. This is why the American poet Robert Bly believes that the real work of men is grief. What does he mean by this? Surely this is a surprising assertion to many of us. Bly is emphasizing that if we are to live wholeheartedly in the present, we must let go of the losses of the past in whatever form they have caused us grief. Many of us mask our grief through anger, overwork, addictions, or anxiety. Real grief work is about mourning our many losses (e.g., innocence, ideals, betrayal, and rejection). For many men, this grief may take the form of a ritual expression or communal lamentation—done in the safety and security of a supportive group—that allows the man to express his grief in an embodied way. Trusting the wisdom of an embodied expression of one's deep emotions is foreign to many men, but it can be a newfound avenue of energy and freedom.

All of us, and certainly the men of whom I am speaking, carry unnamed yearnings and desires of the heart. I suspect that most women are more tuned into this area than are most men. James Hillman has observed that an illness causes the most suffering until it is named correctly. Many of these yearnings can be traced to energetic forces within a man that coalesce around particular images, which we call "archetypal images." Masculine development occurs in distinct stages. Honoring these stages is not at the forefront of most men's minds. Many anthropologists point out the desperate need for Western humanity to reclaim traditional rites of passage for males as they move through these recognized stages of development. One way of entering this realm of initiation is through the archetypes. An archetype is a way of reading human reality through images. Traditionally these images have been presented through larger-than-life stories called *myths*. Depending upon the developmental rite of passage, the most common male archetypes are identified as Hero, Warrior, Lover, Magician, King, and Wise Elder. Embedded within these archetypes is deep cultural wisdom that communities and individuals can tap into for understanding their own maturing growth within Western society. Robert Moore and Douglas

Gillette have written extensively on this aspect in *King, Warrior, Magician, Lover*.

For the boy or young adolescent, the focus is usually on the *Hero* archetype. The heroic impulse is the call to live out the highest ideals of the human person. It is a unifying work that suffuses life's adventures with meaning. Joseph Campbell has written about the way in which this hero journey of the young boy or adolescent enhances the whole of the human community through the individual accomplishment of challenging tasks.

For the young man or the man in midlife, the attention shifts to a different set of archetypes. The *Warrior* is about the discipline or sacrifice necessary for the greater good or ideals of the community. The *Lover* is about the joy, delight, beauty, and relatedness of all creation. The *Magician* is about wisdom, creativity, and transformation of opposites into something new and viable. The *King* is all about power, blessing, expansiveness, and vision for the kingdom. Jesus models for us the image of a balanced man who carries this energy from within and lives from that place of authenticity.

For the older man, the emphasis is on the *Wise Elder* archetype. This represents the inner strength of presence to all of reality with integrity and dignity. It is the place of truth, peace, and goodness. Elijah models this archetype for us.

It should be obvious from this summary that for each archetype there will also be a dark or negative side—the heroic journey can turn into recklessness, the lover can be corrupted into an addict, the magician can become sadistic and narcissistic, the king can become a dictator, and the elder can retreat into his own corner of self-absorption.

A good way of looking at these archetypes is through movies and their characters. Blockbuster movies tend to focus on more than one archetype, which is why they usually draw larger audiences. Some good examples include the Arthurian legends, vampire stories, the Harry Potter series, but best of all is *Star Wars*. *Star Wars* was a new way of engaging this symbol system by reaching out to the unknown expanse of space. So here we have the classic story of good overcoming evil, interfacing with the contemporary imagination, using traditional images. The heroic impulse is primarily carried by Luke and Leia. Luke Skywalker is also the Warrior trained by Yoda the Elder, while Obi-Wan Kenobi is the Magician working against Darth Vader, the dark or evil King. Hans Solo is the lover of self, Leia, money, and adventure.

It's not all that hard. If it's done with genuine companionship, solidarity, creative imagination, and a measure of faith, along with solid reading and formational opportunities, the epic journey of manhood is then a transformative experience in which the boy and the adolescent become a fully developed human being.

Chapter 8
ALL IN THE FAMILY

Finding Your Place
at the Table

I AM THE eldest of eleven children—nine boys and two girls. We grew up playing and fighting as boys always do, but in maturity, we have found a wonderful harmony of spirit, and each year we enjoy our annual Sibling Weekend where we come together, without our spouses and families, to simply enjoy each other's company and have fun. We generally rent a house for four days; we tell stories, play games, ride bikes, hike, we walk on the beach or in the hills, we eat and drink, and we laugh together.

But we are all very different. Like all families, we have developed distinct personalities, varying beliefs, divergent political ideas, and a variety of life philosophies. We certainly do not all march to the same tune. Among the eleven, political leanings range along the continuum from conservative to liberal; religiously we cover ground, including Evangelical, devoutly Catholic, Baptist, not religiously affiliated but "spiritual," Buddhist leanings, and generic Christian. And then there is me—the Catholic priest! We inhabit different socioeconomic levels, and we have different perceptions of what it means to be spiritual. So how did we get here, coming from a deeply devotional Catholic family that was intimately involved in parish life, prayer groups, Church social activities, and all of us the product of an extensive Catholic education?

Clearly, there was a move, for many of us, away from the growing-up process within traditional Catholicism. In this, we are like many families in America, indeed, in the Western world.

Religion should reflect the truth about humanity. At this time, the Catholic Church does not do this as accurately as we might hope. The hierarchy is trapped in a conservative stance that does not allow for the prophetic or progressive very well at all. In any organization, the management or hierarchy certainly has a role in conserving the tradition and holding the center, but if the prophetic and progressive challenge from the periphery is shut out or silenced, then atrophy sets in. This situation is often quoted by people who have become disillusioned with the Catholic Church and walked away, either seeking an alternative tradition or abandoning the practice of Christianity all together.

Much has been written about why people leave the Church. Different statistics, surveys, anecdotes, and proclamations offer varying perspectives on the situation. I would like to introduce another dimension: the imaginal. When people say that they are agnostic, it is probably not so much a lack of belief; rather, it is an inability to accept a tradition or set of beliefs that has not been explained thoroughly or with real intelligent depth. This view is well expressed by Bishop Robert Barron of Los Angeles in his talks and his writings. Faith and spirituality must be taken within a proper context. We live within a postmodern context that is hyper-individualistic and imbued with a strong scientific influence, which translates as "Everything can be explained." That which cannot be explained is dismissed. The confusion ensues when people put science on the same level with the imaginal, the home for faith. Both are to be valued in their own right, but they are two separate categories, viewing reality through a different set of lenses. Science explains reality, while the imaginal teaches us how to live in reality with meaning. There is a valid place for each perspective. Think of when you have had a dream, for example. For you, this might have been a powerful interior experience that reverberates within your memory. For outsiders, this was not an observable event or experience that they can share. The imaginal dream experience can often be deepened when psychoanalysis helps to unpack the meaning of the dream.

Both perspectives can suffer from a shortsightedness or fundamentalism when the other side is denied or disrespected for its unique contribution. Scientific rigor can slip into scientism where literal reality is all that is important, and religion can descend into superstition and paranoia when scientific input is ignored. The mythical imagination invites us to go deeper into the human story and discover the meaning of our lives and the reality in which we are immersed. Science is interested in understanding physical reality, while myth is focused on finding and experiencing meaning. Science studies and evaluates literal reality (the specifics), while the imaginal realm plays with, and dreams of, symbolic expressions (the overarching themes).

A scriptural metaphor might help clarify the difference. In John 13:1–16, at the Last Supper, Jesus washes the feet of his disciples. This was a deeply significant event within the cultural context of his time. The scientific approach would ask all the necessary cultural, historical, and literal questions, such as the following: Did this event actually happen? Who was there? Why did he do this? The answers to these questions help to ground the story in reality. They bring clarity and breadth to the story and help readers of the story and practitioners of the faith to feel a bit of comfort knowing that it is historically accurate in its detail. Liturgically, this event is then carried on through the tradition. The imaginal perspective helps the reader to go deeper into the meaning and significance of the story in order to personalize it. This could be seen as an invitation for each of us to live a life of service for others, no matter what their state in life. At some level, this was achieved by the fact that for several centuries the washing of the feet was celebrated as a sacrament in itself; a living encounter with the risen Christ. A fundamentalist approach to this story would be to argue over whether the feet of women, lapsed Catholics, or nonbelievers could be washed.

Religious maturity invites us to hold both perspectives, the scientific and the imaginal, with equal reference and attention. They enhance each other. Without the scientific approach to life, we can slip into a naive understanding about the cosmos; without the imaginal perspective, life can become sterile and predictable. Holding both perspectives together, we encounter reality with awe, wonder, and gratitude.

Atheism is a relatively new phenomenon in human history, appearing only during the Age of Enlightenment. As humankind began to grapple with the bigger scientific questions of life, there was a gradual separation from the imaginal realm and a fuller embrace and fascination with scientific studies. In my pastoral experience, atheists are often intelligent people who have rejected simplistic perceptions of reality, nonsensical religious devotions, or incomplete images of the Divine. German philosopher and anthropologist Ludwig

Feuerbach, himself an atheist, argued that God was a human invention, a spiritual device to help us deal with our fears and aspirations. This was bad news because human beings projected all their good qualities onto God and saw him as compassionate, wise, loving, and so on, while they saw themselves as greatly inferior. The gods that religion proffers are inconsistent with their experience. Evolutionary biologist and author Richard Dawkins says it this way: We are all atheists about most of the gods that humanity has ever believed in. Some of us just go one god further.

As we read religious history, we notice the many incongruities, inconsistencies, and misguided ideas that Church leadership has offered the people of God. Is it any wonder that many people leave the Church for other venues? These venues include, but are not limited to, other religions, other Christian denominations, or agnosticism/atheism. British comedian and media personality Ricky Gervais says, "It's a strange myth that atheists have nothing to live for. It's the opposite. We have nothing to die for; we have everything to live for." This, then, is the crux of their spirituality: living a life filled with a different set of values.

Everyone has a belief system of one sort or another. It is a way of creating meaning out of the details of our lives. We have, among others, humanists, freethinkers, skeptics, dissenters, Twelve Steppers, and atheists/agnostics. The religious archetype can also be filled with other equally passionate value systems such as sports, politics, gaming, organizations, the military, or nationalism. The place of the imagination is fertile ground for this type of tribal identity and connection. Some questions that can help people to discern if their belief system is authentically assisting them in their own development and maturity are these:

- Does your religion serve you, or do you serve your religion?
- Does your belief system help you to attain the wholeness/happiness you seek, or do you find yourself feeling guilty for all that you have done, not done, or forgotten to do?
- Do your spiritualty and spiritual practices connect you with others or are they self-serving?

These questions may sound revolutionary, but they are the kind that Jesus reflected on. It was from this place of his lived experience that he created his gospel message and a new way of living beyond a tribal mentality. Healthy religion is not about becoming more narrow-minded or judgmental; rather, it is about becoming more broad-minded and welcoming of others—more open than closed. It is not about belonging to a smaller community, but ever larger, expanding communities. The danger for the religious elite is to focus on small liturgical niceties and forget the large matters for living. Jesus spoke to matters of meaning and depth, not function.

Last year our sibling group rented a house in Cayucos on the central coast of California. The house was on the beach, and this opened lots of opportunities for long walks, for sitting around a fire pit, and for conversations around the large kitchen table. There was room for private one-on-one conversations, as well as big and robust discussions. I was eager to talk to my siblings about the religious diversity that had emerged in our family, and this four-day weekend provided sacred space and time for us to exchange views and share our beliefs in a safe setting.

All in the Family

Here are some of the questions that were percolating in my mind over the years as I saw several my brothers and sisters moving away from the Catholic Church.

1. Why did you leave the Catholic Church?
2. What do you miss the most, if anything?
3. What do you find in your present situation that feeds you, that you did not experience in Catholicism?
4. How important is Christian social teaching to you (the common good, reception of strangers, and compassion for the poor)?
5. How has the clergy abuse crisis affected your view of your own Church?
6. What are your frustrations about your Church?
7. How is all this playing out in your children's lives and beliefs?

The path taken by my youngest brother, David, has presented a challenge to my thinking. Brought up and educated, like all of us, as a thoroughgoing Catholic, he now self identifies as not belonging to any religion. Following a major trauma in his life, David found a robust and effective path to healing through his exposure to the teachings and practices of Scientology. As an analytical person, he now finds his truth and guidance through various religious and philosophical sources. He overcame huge physical, mental, and emotional odds, and his faith and determination have been an inspiration to all of us. I must acknowledge that in this miracle of transformation, somehow God is at work. I believe in a God of healing, strength, and power, and that is what I have seen in this twenty-year journey of resurrection by my much younger brother. I have learned much from David. So—why did David leave? He still cherishes Catholic social teaching but quoted his dissatisfaction with a lack of hospitality, of nourishment, of connection with society and its real issues, and finally, judgmentalism. Today he is a man who has grown into integrity, strength, and a fierce determination to live his life to the full. Isn't that what we all want?

This is often how life is. We find ourselves struggling with the effects of trauma, the death of a loved one, or an irregular relationship, which present us with new questions. The old answers no longer fit us or the context of our life. Where life meets belief, we are confronted with an invitation: Do you hold onto something that no longer fits you, for the sake of comfort or out of fear, or do you launch out into the unknown to follow an inner sense of God's guidance, the voice of love and courage? Maturity necessitates that we find a new way or a broader path to embrace the present reality, for no one size of faith or religion fits everyone. There is no one way to experience God or the Divine Presence, or religion, or Church. In my family, we were all "indoctrinated"—in the best sense—to the Roman Catholic worldview through many years of education. Catholicism was the entry portal for all of us. The word *educate* comes from the Latin word *educare*, which means to be led out of, or to train or mold. We learned how to think for ourselves and to discern the trajectory of our lives. This gave each of us a solid foundation and a strong moral consciousness that is evidenced by our career paths. This involves knowing when to move from a smaller worldview into a larger cosmic sense of reality. This has certainly been true for most of my siblings.

All in the Family

I have two sisters, both of whom are very precious to me, but who have taken different paths in their spiritual development. Mary Lou, who lives in Texas, left the Catholic Church because she did not feel connected or fulfilled. She is now a nondenominational Christian who takes her faith very seriously. Her faith community is marked by vibrant worship, preaching, Scripture teaching, and strong fellowship and sharing. This church community has been very supportive to Mary Lou through some difficult challenges in her life.

Virginia, too, takes her faith very seriously. She is a deeply traditional Catholic. Her spirituality is of the immanent variety, in that she calls on God in all the details of her life. She often calls one or more of us to inform us that she has been thinking about us and praying for us very specifically. Virginia frequently asks me for reading recommendations or explanations of the faith. It has been exciting to see her explore the more expansive horizons of Catholicism.

Tony, who is the closest brother in age to me, left the Catholic Church some years ago due to disillusionment with several pastors of parishes he had attended. He simply did not find the spiritual nurture and challenge that he was seeking, nor the relevance necessary to his life. He briefly followed his wife into a church in the Evangelical tradition, but now finds great consolation and support in some of the best contemporary Christian authors, some of whom are Catholic. In addition, he has discovered several helpful Buddhist authors and practices. He is particularly drawn to meditation. Tony no longer identifies with Catholicism.

Daniel and Larry feature in the family as the most zealous and publicly expressive in their faith. Both attend Evangelical churches and their guiding light is Scripture, which they look to for their moral and spiritual centering. Both left Catholicism for similar reasons: there was, in their experience, no depth or preparation in the homilies or teaching on Scripture, or other opportunities for solid adult enrichment. This is often the case when clergy do not practice the necessary discipline of preparation and commitment to adult faith enrichment. For many people, religion in its current form is not helping, but rather is impeding, people's spiritual progress and development.

Tom has left the regular practice of Catholicism because of what he considered an excessive emphasis on rules that seems to lose sight of the original kerygma or gospel proclamation of Jesus. He considers himself spiritual, not religious, and practices daily prayer and meditation. While he misses the eucharistic sharing, he takes solace in his family and friends as his primary community support.

My brother John is a practicing Catholic who has lost respect for the institution because of the clergy abuse scandal. He sees this as a leadership crisis, in which many of the bishops have not protected the flock. John is nourished by a sense of shared experience, whether it is through the Eucharist or quietly helping others.

Paul is a traditional Catholic who takes his commitment very seriously. A former Marine, he finds he experiences spiritual growth through his personal prayer life. This includes a regular practice of meditation and creating life-giving rituals. His many years of faithful participation in spiritual direction have also served to enhance this growth. Like John, Paul thinks that we have a crisis of institutional leadership citing leadership failure (lack of connection with the people, the abuse crisis, and boring liturgies).

Peter is a man who leans into different spiritual traditions, depending upon the context. To my mind, he is a good example of those people who describe themselves as spiritual, not religious. As an adolescent, he found himself rebelling against the religion that was "forced upon" him. Now it seems that he has come full circle and is reclaiming some of the lessons and experiences that sustained him when he was younger. Peter misses the communal worship and song as well as his former involvement in social action. At present, he finds his connection to men's groups very fulfilling. He does his best to be faithful to his belief in God and to seek God's will in his life. As a long-distance truck driver, he regularly asks his siblings for prayer for safe traveling and guidance.

We are a kind of religious United Nations. And I haven't even mentioned the in-laws or the next generation of Clarkes!

Though we have come from the same parents and grew up in the same house, we have different emotional, psychological, and intellectual needs. It seems obvious to me that God delights in diversity. Whether it is in reading the Scriptures, observing nature, studying anthropology, or reading history, I am fascinated by the diverse ways and means that God uses to get across this message. We humans tend to be tribal, while God is not. God is about community and connections, building bridges between all that is, reminding us that everything belongs in one way or another.

Chapter 9

WALKING WITH JESUS—OR TRAVELING FIRST CLASS IN COMFORT?

I WAS FIRST introduced to the Household of Faith Charismatic Community in Los Angeles through a weekend retreat experience that I was asked to facilitate for the group at a local retreat center. Over the years, I have worked with and genuinely enjoyed being a part of this dynamic group of people. They are predominantly a Catholic Filipino group of all ages, fully engaged in individual Catholic practices such as daily Eucharist, Scripture reading, personal prayer, and Marian devotions. They are actively engaged in their own parishes but travel from all parts of the archdiocese to participate in their Friday evening prayer group. There are numerous groups of this kind that have sprung up throughout the world since the 1970s in response to a felt need for a deeper personal connection with God. Charismatic prayer groups have made a huge contribution to the Church since Vatican II (1962–65). The contemporary renewal began in 1967 as a lay movement of students from Duquesne University who desired to connect and actively experience the power of the Holy Spirit in their lives. As with any renewal movement, it became a niche for individuals looking to deepen or experience their faith, not just through their intellect, but also through their emotions.

In 1996, I was asked to organize and oversee the charismatic prayer groups of the Archdiocese of Los Angeles. This was no small task, as this responsibility involved facilitating the training and guidance of people from several cultural traditions. It was a rare privilege that gave me a unique opportunity to view the Catholic experience outside my own cultural background and experience. After overcoming overwhelming anxiety and self-doubt, I leapt into the challenge with zeal and determination. I began by reflecting on my own charismatic experience and conversion at the age of seventeen, which brought me back to the emotional grounding of why I was still a Catholic. The charismatic experience deeply formed my personal relationship with Jesus, empowered by the Spirit. This heartfelt relationship nourished my faith life throughout my adulthood and into my priestly ministry. The charismatic prayer groups and leadership experiences gave me a necessary communal bonding and sense of personal commitment that expanded into more responsible positions of authority. At the same time, I remember feeling alienated from the institutional Church and could not understand the reason for so many rules and rubrics. Why not just pray and listen to the guidance of the Spirit and do God's will? I know that I was not alone with these questions.

Looking today at the big picture of this genre of prayer group, I know that because of years of education and ministerial experience, I now have a broader perspective to offer people in similar circumstances. Laypeople often feel left out of the loop in terms of adult faith formation and deeper prayer experiences, not to mention a sense of exclusion in ecclesial leadership and decision-making. I have found that many lay-people respond to this feeling of being sidelined by Church leadership by practicing what they perceive as accessible devotions, which seem to meet their faith needs. Devotions invariably are about connecting our creedal belief system with our heart or emotional attachment. There are countless devotions and prayer forms to choose from: the Rosary, the Divine Mercy chaplet, novenas, litanies to various saints, Centering Prayer, intercessions, reading of Scripture, Marian devotions, and so on. Each has its own place in tradition and practice, according to the time and context of our particular life situation. But danger often occurs when the context is separated from the devotion.

Prayer and devotions are meant to expand our experience of the Divine, not shrink it. Without an external guide or support network to offer an objective perspective on our progress, we can slip into practicing a multiplicity of devotions rather than focusing on growing in the life of virtue. All prayer and devotion is meant to aid us in this pursuit. When it comes to devotional practices, there is a simple guideline to remember: quality is much more important than quantity. Repeating numerous prayers or countless mantras will not get God's attention as much as will a heart aligned with the will of God (Matt 7:21). Once I met a woman who was "attending" daily Eucharist and had set out a variety of holy cards on the pew next to her. She proceeded to read (pray) each of the prayers on the cards silently while Mass was going on. Clearly, she wanted to incorporate all her prayer routines into one. This is a gross misunderstanding of what prayer is meant to do for us and through us. The purpose of prayer is to remind us of our connection to God and to change the way we relate to reality. In this way, we grow in the life of virtue. This necessitates a focus of our mind and heart on God. The prayer form is merely the means to assist this process. A diffused awareness, however, can create distractions and can lead to frustration and possible scrupulosity.

Msgr. Tony Doherty, an Australian priest with a rich history of faithful service, describes prayer this way: "Prayer is not the fashioning of unfamiliar, stumbling words to a distant God; Prayer is not some form of magic or merely the delusions of a frightened people. Prayer is actually a form of loving. It is a rich juicy language of love: love of the astonishing gift of this planet, love of the people who have touched our lives, love of the mystery that has given us life and embraces us throughout our journey" (Piper and Doherty, *The Attachment*). Yes, this is what real prayer is, the prayer of the human heart.

Christian prayer seeks to bring together our whole person before God: head, heart, and body. Nothing is beyond God's interest. We each have our own unique personalities and preferences, and this will be reflected in our prayer. Some prefer heartfelt prayer while others prefer more intellectual practices, and others choose to focus on embodied forms of spiritual expression. Each has its place in the economy of our faith life. My friend Joan has no heart experience of God, but she finds great consolation and support in her intellectual pursuit of spiritual reading. Another friend, Joe, is highly intuitive and thoroughly enjoys charismatic prayer. My friend Maria is deeply moved by music and ritual. Yet another friend, Jack, takes great delight in long-distance running. He calls it his contemplative practice. To each his/her own!

It might help to note, again, that each form of prayer is a means to connect with the Creator. When the method gets in the way of this intimate connection, change is needed. Often we might find that breakthroughs happen when we change

our method. I remember one time when I was stuck emotionally in an area of my professional life. I had been praying in
my normal heartfelt way and seeking God's guidance. I had
also been talking with some trusted friends about what to do
and even doing some reading on the topic, but there was no
change. I just felt blocked, overwhelmed, and consumed by
darkness. Then a wise priest mentor suggested I try creating
a personal ritual. That embodied prayer experience changed
my whole outlook and gave me a new release and energy in
my life.

When the head, heart, and body are aligned, there is a
power, an energy of congruence that affirms God's will and
direction in our life. Prayer is a part of this work of helping
us to regularly live in the true alignment of our personhood.
Remember that behavioral work must be matched by attitudi-
nal change; otherwise, it remains inauthentic. This is the core
message of the Christian commandments—we call them "The
Beatitudes"—as enunciated by Jesus. What helps you to live in
your authentic personality? What forms of prayer or spiritual
practices help you to pay attention to your whole humanity in
relation to the Creator?

When our psychology (our self-understanding) and our
spirituality (our understanding of God) become separated
from the reality of our identity, then we can be drawn into various forms of superstition. An impoverished theology leads to
an impoverished experience of myself. Usually this strikes us
at our weakest moments, or times of powerlessness. This can
take the form of "special" prayers or practices that are "guar-
anteed" to change God's mind or to get God to do something
for us. Their genesis is often questionable but highly credible
to people in emotional turmoil. They can also take the form
of "promises" to God through extreme physical practices (e.g.,

crawling on one's knees for a great distance, being flagellated or crucified in a public display of religious fervor, burying a statue of St. Joseph upside down in order to sell one's house in a timely manner, medieval superstitions, etc.). What all of these practices ignore is the relational aspect of God's love for us. Superstition is about trying to control God, while faith is about trust in God. God desires the best for us in an adult, straightforward manner. There is no need to jump through hoops, physically punish oneself, dance or move a certain way, or even to sing on key! Rather God wants a heart set right with God and with all people. What practice will help you to do that?

One of the great strengths of the Charismatic Movement, as I have experienced it, is the communal aspect of bonding through prayer and worship. Charismatics tend to gather in prayer groups and prayer communities to experience regular support for their encounters with the Holy Spirit. Singing, praying aloud or in silence, prepared teachings, prayer for members in need, and testimonies of God's action in their lives are a normal part of the prayer group gathering. One of the dangers is that these groups can become more culturally or ethnically focused rather than focusing on the faith of the adherents. Questions that these groups need to answer if they are to remain faithful to the Tradition are the following: Is everyone welcome? Is the exclusive use of English (or Tagalog or Spanish or Korean) excluding some people? What is the relationship of this group with the larger parish and broader community? Is there any oversight or input from an authorized spiritual director?

Without proper care and pastoral leadership, these types of prayer groups can easily suffer from leadership dysfunction. In my experience, the prayer groups that suffered the most were the ones without a wise and knowledgeable leader who was professionally connected with the Archdiocese. The following are some of the leadership issues that I have witnessed in my years of ministry:

- Corruption and nepotism
- Functional atheism
- Misuse of money
- Unhealthy liaisons
- Unwillingness to face issues of the human shadow
- Misunderstanding of the place of the devil in salvation
- Lack of theological expertise
- A heavy-handed hierarchal model of leadership
- Power issues
- Lack of proper oversight
- Unwillingness to face reality
- Lack of psychological awareness

One of the weaknesses of the Charismatic Renewal is its lack of focus on social mercy and social justice. This movement tends to focus on an individualistic approach or "super-spiritual" way to salvation, rather than including all of God's people in works of justice and peace. This can put adherents at odds with their pastors, who would like to see them more involved in outreach services.

Some individuals are drawn to public displays of spiritual gifts such as miracles, physical healing, prophecy, and speaking in tongues (1 Cor 12:4–11). These are manifestations of the Spirit in a situation. They are not necessarily a sign of holiness in an individual. The gifts are meant to invite the recipients into

83

a deeper relationship with the Giver. In contrast, the fruits of the Holy Spirit (Gal 5:22–23) are signs of the growing presence of God's maturing work within a person. This divine work is often hidden in the interior of one's own soul. Many of these members have been blessed with ordinary mystical experiences of the Divine. Their growth is measured in their virtuous life and avoidance of obvious vices.

Healing is manifested in a variety of ways: physical, emotional, spiritual, relational, psychological. A healing occurs when a person notices a temporary cessation or a lessening of the intensity of the suffering. A cure happens when the lingering ailment disappears completely and does not reappear. A deliverance is a form of healing in which the person experiences a spiritual release from evil spirits or inclinations. Often a person's illness is more complicated that it appears. For this reason, in many cases, the healing approach should be multifaceted, with the involvement of professional oversight and discernment. This is especially true with family relationships and marital struggles. It is not unheard of for prayer group members to turn to intercessory prayer or the blessing of one's family house as the sole means for relational healing. This can border on superstition.

Many of us can sometimes forget that private devotions or pious practices are to be subservient to the public belief system of our religion. Healthy devotions are to assist us to be more fully immersed in this life, not to escape this life for the next. For how we live this moment is how we live forever. Any one of us can be misled by our misplaced or misguided religious enthusiasm. For this reason, Christianity has a long history of respecting the need for wise spiritual direction and spiritual counsel in these matters. Visions, apparitions, locutions, and spiritual gifts are to be placed at the feet of wise healthy leadership for discernment. Without this process we are confronted with the sight of well-meaning people kneeling to receive communion and making all manner of show around the eucharistic experience. We need to get back to the original agenda of Jesus. This agenda includes, but is not limited to, doing something different in our lives, not in the temple! Most conversion stories in the gospel took place outside the temple proper and in the daily lives of people. This is an important biblical understanding in that the Sunday experience is meant to change the way we live the rest of the week. When we forget this truth, we can slip into numerous devotional practices as an escape from reality, rather than becoming more deeply immersed into the mystery of our lives and our relationship with God!

Often, we can forget—or never understand—the original reason some traditional religious devotions developed. When this happens, we can easily be led down a path that steers us away from the meaning significance of the devotion. All devotions can be summarized in a single theme or sentence. This is why we are encouraged to reflect on the devotions and their meaning for us individually, so that we can apply it to our life. Let's look at a few of these devotions.

Eucharistic processions were started in the early fourteenth century to draw the faithful's attention to the power and authority of Christ in our midst. The pomp and circumstance reflected the pageantry surrounding the emperor or king's role in secular society. This devotion was a way of balancing the power between the heavenly and the earthly realms. Does this devotion have a place in today's postmodern society? That is a good question. Some pastors believe it does. However, I would like to point out that it is most important to maintain the theme, not the pageantry, to be authentically devotional.

Otherwise, the practice becomes more important than the meaning of the event.

Another popular devotion begun in the fourth century is the pilgrimage. Originally, this devotion was twofold: to help the devotee connect with God via the holy places in Europe and the Middle East, and to connect with one's own interior life. The community supported the pilgrimage experience. Nowadays, a pilgrimage has essentially become a holiday trip, often with no expense spared and no real sacrifice offered by the pilgrim.

I would also like to address the tradition of praying novenas. This practice began relatively early in the Church as a way of connecting with the apostles' wait in Jerusalem between the Ascension and Pentecost as they prayed for the coming of the Holy Spirit. This period was nine days, hence a novena. The time has been traditionally marked with a sustained period of prayer for a specific intention. Over the years, this prayer focus has been diverted to Mary and specific saints to acquire the answer to a prayer intention. Perhaps we need to return to the original fervor of waiting for the coming of the Spirit, not knowing what is to come. This is a stance of powerlessness and meekness, not one of power and trying to control God.

Finally, it is helpful to remember that veneration of the Blessed Virgin Mary and the saints must be properly aligned with the worship of God. Too often well-meaning, faith-filled individuals place more importance on their favorite saint or Marian devotion (often through a veiled form of nationalism) than on the Creator of us all. This sets up a very unbalanced approach to life in which we tend to canonize others and infantilize ourselves. The Church identifies the lives of many different personalities who elevate the ideals of our humanity to such a degree that we call them "holy." The stories of these people, who have overcome a variety of challenges, are meant to inspire us to live out our own lives in deeply fulfilling and meaningful ways. Through these examples, God invites us to take up the cross of responsibility for our own life and live our lives in a mature, compassionate way, caring for others in their need.

The people of the charismatic prayer groups, whose spiritual longings I honor and respect, have much to offer the Catholic community if they can embrace wholeheartedly the broad Catholic economy of social justice, open community, social mercy, and strong bonds with the local and the universal Church.

Chapter 10
WE'RE NOT REALLY RELIGIOUS, BUT...

OVER THE YEARS, I have had the privilege of visiting various places in Australia and have developed many lasting friendships. Both my work and my vacations have provided me with many opportunities to observe Australians in their cultural milieu. While I am neither a sociologist nor anthropologist, I find it helpful and interesting to compare cultures and their value systems. As a result of my work and social interactions, I often find myself reflecting on the experience of Australians and their way of life.

Unlike America, Australia does not inhabit a religious culture. No assertions of "in God we trust," "One nation under God," or anything similar. Religion has not generally featured in public utterances or discourse or political campaigns. Nonetheless, I find that here, in reputedly the most secular nation on earth, deeply spiritual questions frequently swirl through social, familial, and community gatherings. The Aussie barbeque is the quintessential setting for the emergence of these questions.

Recently, the Australian government conducted a nation-wide judicial proceeding called a Royal Commission. The purpose was to examine and shine a powerful light on the problem of the sexual abuse of children by institutions, individuals, churches, and other bodies, including sporting bodies. The Royal Commission presented a dismaying review of the Catholic Church's participation in and cover-up of these abuses. It has been a lengthy and painful experience for the whole country but extremely cathartic. The process has been carried out objectively with respect and concern for all participants. This was not a "religion bashing" event nor was it a "witch hunt." It was truth seeking resolution and reconciliation. As you can imagine, this topic has been written about extensively, and discussed publicly on radio and television, as well as through social media. It also is brought up often in private circles of family and friends. At least partly because of this national process, religion has now intruded into the barbeque conversation of Australians. This is a new development in this country, as religion is not a topic for social or public conversation as it is in the United States. There is a sharp cultural difference here. Australia is an unabashedly secular country founded by men of the Enlightenment. They wanted religion kept out of government, yet there has historically been a genuine attempt at social justice, best exemplified in a universal health care system and a robust commitment of public funding of religious schools. Yes, there is a dearth of public religious experience in Australia, but Australians generally have a sense of egalitarianism, that everyone should have a "fair go."

Because of the shame and embarrassment as a result of this highly publicized investigation, in general, it is not comfortable for people to identify as Catholic. As of this writing, slightly less than 10 percent of Australian Catholics regularly practice their faith now. However, my experience has taught me that though Australians are not religious in the traditional sense, they are, in fact, spiritual in terms of their overall values and concern for social and humanitarian issues. They do not frequent retreats or spiritual gatherings. For the majority, religion is a private issue, not a public declaration. Last year I was present at a barbeque in the Melbourne area with my close friends who come from a variety of political persuasions and career paths. We had a robust and engaging discussion around several topics from politics to religion to sports. People generally do engage in debate about civil and social issues without shouting down those with different opinions.

The situation of the Aborigines and the treatment of refugees is a good example of this ongoing debate in the public and private sectors of society. Pope Francis has regularly spoken out about the moral imperative to protect migrants "and among these particularly men and women in irregular situations," as well as those "exiled and seeking asylum" or "victims of trafficking." Moreover, he said, "defending their inalienable rights, ensuring their fundamental freedoms and respecting their dignity are duties from which no one can be exempted" (Sixth International Forum on Migration and Peace, February 21–22, 2017). There is a deep angst among many people about Australia's treatment of refugees and the native Aborigines. This is not religion based as much as it is based on an authentic humanitarian instinct. Because of the relatively small size of the population of this country (roughly twenty-five million people), this topic has serious ramifications for the whole society. The sociological phenomenon of "otherness" is alive and well. "Othering" is a social process that perpetuates negative stereotypes. It is a political tool that many in positions of power can use to hold the moral high ground.

Identity and social belonging are as fragile in Australia as anywhere else, but my observation is that debate around these issues tends to be generally open and civilized. The clash of cultures and religious practices of refugees and asylum seekers with the dominant value system has sometimes created an unstable, and in some cases, violent environment. I have been impressed with the public discussion about this important postmodern challenge: How do we compassionately and adequately create a new global community that respects and honors each culture without sacrificing the community's need for order and safety? Again, Pope Francis reminds us as we face this paradoxical question that "we have a duty toward our brothers and sisters who, for various reasons, have been forced to leave their homeland: a duty of justice, of civility, and of solidarity" (Forum on Migration and Peace).

Perhaps we can learn from the Australians' struggles how to address our own challenges with our rising homeless populations both nationally and globally. This also blends into the discussion on refugees and immigration policies. As Pope Francis has repeatedly reminded us, we must avoid leading with our tribal or nationalistic tendencies, which can easily devolve into an individualistic approach to religion and to humanity. Religion at its best is a call to move from paranoia (deep unprocessed fear) to metanoia (waking up to a new way of seeing). We seem to have forgotten that we belong to each other. Elitism at any level of society is just not acceptable. There are no easy answers to these overwhelming human and economic challenges. Perhaps we could take a lesson from some of the ritual practices of the First Nation peoples in listening more carefully to each other's stories without judgment, so that we can find a common ground on which to resolve this postmodern problem. Many of the First Nation peoples use a practice that has come to be called the "Way of Council." This is a communal method that creates the discipline of listening and speaking to one another without interruption or denigration. It seeks a way to seek a common ground to resolve differences. The basic guidelines are these:

- The participants sit in a well-defined circle where everyone can clearly see one another.
- There is a sacred center in which a mat is placed on the ground. On the mat is a singing bowl or gong, along with a talking stick and a candle.
- The process begins with someone making a prayer or dedication and then lighting the candle. Others can add their own prayers or dedications separately and then conclude by lightly striking the bowl.
- The leader then reminds the participants of the simple guidelines:
  1. Speak from the heart.
  2. Listen from the heart.
  3. Be spontaneous.
  4. Be lean of expression.
     - There is no crosstalk or intervention; only mutual respect and confidentiality.
     - When a person wants to speak, he must hold the talking stick while all others listen. At the conclusion of an individual sharing, all respond with a verbal assent (e.g., "I hear you").
     - Everyone gets a chance to speak.

- The process continues until the allotted time is concluded.

As this process unfolds, it is almost magical to observe how the group creates a more open and cohesive environment. The participants may not agree with each other's comments, but they know they have been received with respect and a listening ear.

I know of a Catholic parish where the pastor was struggling with how to bring together a group of Catholic women who held fiercely different viewpoints over Right to Life issues. Both groups were practicing Catholics, but neither group was willing or able to find a way to truly listen to each other. So the pastor invited a woman who was trained in the art of storytelling and conversation to come for a Saturday afternoon "retreat." He then invited both groups of women to the retreat, introduced the speaker, and left for the day. What unfolded was nothing short of a miracle. No one changed their political viewpoint, but all left with a greater respect for each woman's story and their beliefs. Judgmentalism fell by the wayside as they experienced their common humanity and dignity. The danger is that many of our religious leaders would like to rise above it all and not address the real issue at the heart: the fear of the foreign, strange, or different. If we say that, spiritually speaking, everything belongs and everyone has a place in the reality of things, then how do we live from a place of conversion rather than of fear?

As Catholics we are pro-life, from womb to tomb, not just pro-birth. Life is a seamless garment that the Church upholds through its social doctrine grounded on Jesus's words of warning about the last judgment in Matthew 25:31–46: "Amen, I say to you, whatever you did for one of these least brothers [or sisters] of mine, you did for me." Who are the least of your brothers/sisters in your life—the imprisoned, the infirm, the dying, the homeless, the addicted, the migrants, the refugees, the stranger, the hungry? Every one of us is challenged by this doctrinal teaching of Jesus. It is, and should always be, the platform for all our discussions and interpretations of Catholic social teaching.

Today, Pope Francis has focused such discussions on a topic relatively, although not entirely, new to the faithful: climate change and the protection of Mother Earth. Climate change seems to be a topic primarily for the more educated in America, but in Australia, the conversation seems to be more widespread and passionate. Australia is already experiencing the effects of global pollution and mismanagement of environmental resources, including significant degradation of the Great Barrier Reef, which is rightly considered a national, as well as a global natural treasure. Climate is a very emotional topic for many Australians as they are already experiencing more extremes of weather with more severe droughts and higher incidence of skin cancer. The pope has spoken very clearly: "It must be said that some committed and prayerful Christians, with the excuse of realism and pragmatism, tend to ridicule expressions of concern for the environment. Others are passive; they choose not to change their habit and thus become inconsistent. So what they all need is an 'ecological conversion,' whereby the effects of their encounter with Jesus Christ become evident in their relationship with the world around them. Living our vocation to be protectors of God's handiwork is essential to a life of virtue; it is not an optional or a secondary aspect of our Christian experience" (*Laudato Si'* 217).

In the general absence of a national or civic religion, then, where does the accompanying human impulse surface?

I wonder if it is in the sports culture. Australia has a population significantly less than one-tenth of the United States, and yet this large country (in size) regularly plays sports at the highest levels of international completion. At the Olympics, for example, Australia regularly positions itself among the top five countries winning medals. In effect, sports seems to be the national religion of this Southern Hemisphere country. Sports give Australians a large part of their national identity and meaning. The pomp and ceremony (colors, anthems, chants, language) surrounding sports is intriguing to observe. The language is religious in describing the field of play ("the sacred turf," "holy ground),", as is the description of the fans ("devoted followers" of the game). What sports are we talking about? Aussie football, cricket, rugby, tennis, soccer, and volleyball are among the most popular.

One of the functions of religion is to capture and direct human passion; in Australia, the vacuum in public life left by the absence of religion certainly seems to be filled by sports and the surrounding culture. What impact then does this have on the spirituality of a nation? Only time will tell.

Chapter 11

WHERE ARE YOU, GOD, AFTER ALL I'VE DONE FOR YOU?

CORPUS CHRISTI AGED CARE is a well-regarded Catholic facility in a major capital city in Australia. A resident priest chaplain provides daily Mass, holy communion is distributed to those too frail to attend the chapel, and a pastoral care worker visits daily. There is excellent spiritual care.

Margery lives at Corpus Christi. She is a feisty ninety-two-year-old who is bedridden, can no longer read or watch television, and is left alone with her feelings. Her world has shrunk into the memories of her life, with occasional visits from her two sons. And she is very, very angry with God. Almost as angry as she is with his Mother. I met Margery when, by invitation, I visited with the pastoral care worker, who is a friend of mine. "God's abandoned me," was her greeting as my friend introduced us. "Oh?" I replied, thinking privately that this was, at the very least, an interesting opening remark.

"Yes," she continued, "after nearly ninety years of being faithful, working for the Church, going to daily Mass, praying novenas, the Rosary, the Divine Mercy chaplet, marching with the Right to Life, God's abandoned me. Gone. No matter how much I pray or ask for a sign of his presence. Zero."

I had noticed a picture of St. Therese of Lisieux over her bed, and an inspirational thought struck me. "I see you're devoted to St. Therese; you know that she had an experience of darkness toward the end of her life—perhaps you could ask her for her intercession." "Great help she is," retorted Margery, "she's gone too. Along with Mary, and I have been devoted to Mary all my life. I'm angry with them all."

Margery is by no means unique in her pain. Loneliness and feelings of desolation strike most of us at one time or another. It is especially painful when it strikes us at the end of life. How do we begin to unpack these devastating feelings to discover another layer of meaning? Is there nothing or no one strong enough to help us carry this confusing convolution of thoughts and feelings? How do we deal with feelings of betrayal, being let down by God, or abandonment? We are in similar territory here to the landscape described by the sixteenth-century mystic John of the Cross in his poem "The Dark Night of the Soul." The parallels might not be exact, but this state of existential angst is certainly not unknown to vast numbers of believers.

Responses to this experience can vary widely. John of the Cross responded with poetry, silent suffering, and deep contemplative prayer. His much-loved friend, the great St. Teresa of Avila, responded differently when confronted with what she saw as God's failure to step up when she needed him; she responded by publicly informing God that if this was the way he treated his friends, then it was no wonder he had so few!

I suspect most of us, privately at least, would concur with Teresa. Her response has the quality of human honesty and affront, which is, by the way, the hallmark of authentic prayer.

The psalms are fitting examples of this type of honesty (Pss 22, 44, 86, 88). This is the setting for many of the "suffering psalms" of the Bible, also known as Lamentations (1:12–14; 3:1–20). The Book of Job also addresses the suffering of an innocent person. Include with this Jesus's anguish on the cross: "My God, my God, why have you forsaken me?" (Matt 27:46). This is the quintessential example of the human experience of betrayal and abandonment. These prayer expressions are terse and laconic because they come from a place of deep instinctual pain and suffering. In our darkest hours, we can certainly identify with them.

"Christ preached a gospel of universal love and forgiveness, and with that accepted the lethal consequences of that message in first century Roman ruled Palestine. He accepted the full implications of his being a mortal human being. If we respond to this message as generously as possible and accept our own suffering and death, we too will be assured of the triumph of the same resurrection" (Windsor, *The Tempest Tossed Church*, 118).

Remember that there are different templates, metaphors, images, stories, and archetypes to follow as guides to give deeper meaning to our suffering. Choose the one that best fits your situation. For example, how does suffering fit into your paradigm of salvation, or healing, or answered prayer? Do you believe that God hears the prayers only of the righteous, or is it possible that God is communicating with you in a different dialect?

Pain is inevitable; suffering is a choice. Pain is the sensation of the hurt, and suffering is the response to the pain. Usually these two operate in tandem, but often a conscious choice can be made. A woman friend of mine is regularly hurt by one of her daughters, who fails to contact her with cards or phone calls on special occasions. There is no hostility, just an uncaring attitude. The mother eventually made the decision simply not to suffer the ongoing disappointment, reasoning that she had done all she could to be a good mother, but the daughter did not feel intimately connected to her. Acceptance of that situation allowed her to continue to love her daughter, knowing that the power to maintain the relationship was in her hands. Every type of pain is, in effect, an invitation to do something about "what is wrong." How we respond to the pain can be healing, liberating, or enlarging, or it can be constrictive, destructive, or death-dealing. This is why our pain, and pain in general, has much to teach us. What has your pain taught you?

Suffering is meant to change and soften us. C. G. Jung once said, "Neurosis is a good escape from meaningful suffering." To suffer pain wisely is the necessary task of every human being; otherwise, we are cursed to repeat the process countless times with no change. This was the image that Dante used to describe hell—repetitive activity with no ability to modify or alter one's reality. Meaningful suffering is different. It involves discovering a secret deep inside the wound or pain that usually cannot be learned in any other way. What have you learned from your suffering?

We are creatures in an incomplete, evolving cosmos. Suffering has many sources both inner and outer: cosmic, anthropological, psychological, relational, accidental, spiritual, and violent encounters. Suffering confronts us with some of the big questions of life: What is the meaning, value, or worth of my life? What is this all for? Where is God amid this?—Margery's big question. Her pain is especially overwhelming because, as she has said, she did everything that she was told in order to be faithful to God. All the promises that she was given by religious authorities, Scripture, and the Church have proven baseless. She has spent her whole life in service to the God that she worshiped, but in her hour of need, her faith, hope, and love have been wrested from her, with no adequate replacement.

God did not come to take away our pain or suffering, but to stand with us in its midst and to imbue our suffering with meaning. As St. Thomas More famously said, God did not come to suppress suffering, not even to explain it, but to fill it with his Presence. Religion at its best teaches us how to see even in the darkness, how to know what to do with our pain/suffering, and how to transform it. That is why the cross is the central symbol of Christianity; it is the symbol of transformation. The cross reminds us of that process of transformation through Jesus's example. This is a fourfold process:

1. Face the pain humbly and courageously.
2. Hold it and ponder the mystery of it.
3. Accept it.
4. Give back something different in kind.

This is the continuing work of salvation. Salvation (wholeness) is pain, suffering, sorrow, and/or failure confronted and transformed. Where is God inviting you to grieve and mourn your losses? This is the invitation of Good Friday. Easter does not happen without Good Friday. The fruits of this honest confrontation are generosity, healing, and compassion.

There is a real art to suffering with meaning, to collaborate with God in this transformative work. Here are some suggestions:

- Name the moment or experience accurately.
- Ponder the experience.

- Reaffirm the center of your faith (entrust your-self to God).
- Check your vision; we see only what we focus on.
- Engage in embodied movement or expression: artwork, music, poetry, ritual, exercise.
- Use appropriate symbols, images, and meta-phors.
- Connect with Nature.
- Share your story and connect with others in a nonjudgmental way.
- Connect with biblical metaphors (agony in the garden, standing at the foot of the cross).

Walter Brueggemann reminds us that the Scriptures present a threefold pattern in the stories of the patriarchs: First, they were securely oriented, then painfully disoriented, and then surprisingly reoriented. The same is true for each of us. This is the core of the Christian paschal story: living—dying—rising, over and over again. Any way you look at it, this is a difficult, painful, and terrible process that is nevertheless essential to moving forward in the valley of tears.

For Margery to find her way forward, she will have to own the fact that she has an inadequate and incomplete image of God that is tainted with some toxic beliefs; for example, that she can work her way to heaven, and that having a bulletproof faith will protect her from any problem or pain. It also appears that she might have a bit of a religious addiction that serves to help her avoid reality. Margery needs to honestly and com-pletely face her unbearable grief—that she has been betrayed by the very God that she sought to serve. Then she will essen-tially need to accept the unacceptable truth that what gave her meaning before no longer serves her. Reality requires that, recognizing that she is existentially alone, she trust that something new will happen. This is the antithesis of control, which is what Margery has subconsciously lived with all her adult life. She was trying to control God by secretly making a contract with God: I will do this for you (go to Mass for nine successive first Fridays, or seven first Saturdays, make x number of novenas in one year, etc.), but you must do "this" for me. What made this contract especially tragic was that it appeared to be supported by some of our Church teachings.

Of course, God has not abandoned her. God is present in ways that Margery cannot or will not accept. "A life of unbetrayed principles and love took this divine person to death" (Windsor, 137)—and so it will be for Margery. Her cry will be heard just as the cry of Jesus on the cross was heard by his Father, and her pain will indeed be transformed into joy, in God's time, not hers. If only we could control this process, but alas we cannot. We live and die in the hands of the One who loves us beyond our imaginings, and that must be enough for our questioning hearts.

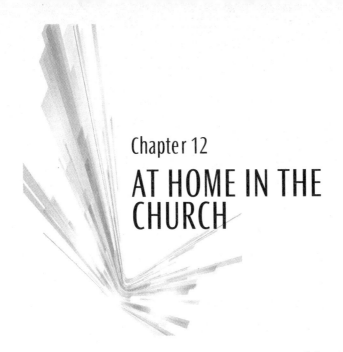

Chapter 12
AT HOME IN THE CHURCH

MARY AND JOSEPH Retreat Center is a peaceful oasis set in extensive gardens, situated on a bluff in Rancho Palos Verdes, California. It is a place of peace and tranquility. I have had both a professional and a personal connection with this lovely retreat center through my maternal aunt, Sr. Maria Immaculata Ottman, who was a professed member of the Daughters of Mary and Joseph for more than seventy-five years. Often, I have been privileged to facilitate retreats here for diverse groups of people looking for spiritual direction, guidance, or professional updating in the field of spirituality. Some are ordinary Catholics who simply want to connect more closely with God; some are catechists, pastoral workers, or volunteers; some are professional Church workers. These folks are seeking to integrate their work and relational life with their spiritual life. One of the perennial themes that I find recurring is that of a sense of "stuckness" in repetitive patterns of thinking and behaving—patterns that people see as restrictive, and which they would like to challenge or change.

But what if we could learn something from these repetitive patterns in our life? What then? I believe that we could reclaim this energy and focus it for greater purposes. Here are some examples of these energetic patterns of thoughts or attitudes that tend to stifle many religious people:

- Compartmentalization: What I do at work or at home has nothing to do with my faith
- Hypocrisy: Saying one thing and doing another
- Secrecy: Living a double life (public vs. private life)
- Gossip: Malicious talk about another person or group so that I feel better about myself or superior to others
- Denial: Repression of instinctual desires instead of integration of these human yearnings. In other words, do they control me, or do I manage them in a way that brings me happiness?
- Deceit: Telling lies to escape the truth of my reality, which disconnects me from my authentic self
- Judgmentalism: Putting people into different categories so I do not have to relate to them as persons

Accepting others and ourselves as we are is a challenging task. It is a necessary, continuing work that is called for in the work of maturity and living out the gospel mandate to love God with our whole being and to love others as ourselves. This is a daily work of forgiveness—letting life be as it is. I call this a spirituality of imperfection—loving imperfect reality as it is. Duns Scotus, the Franciscan philosopher, opined that the particular is the way to the universal. If we want to experience the universal depth of God's life and love in our own lives, then we must learn to love the people that we live with, worship with, and work with, for all are a part of the family of God.

A few years ago, I walked the Camino de Santiago de Compostela pilgrimage in Spain with my friend Fr. Patrick Mullen. It was an enriching experience of faith, friendship, and insight. At the conclusion of our journey, we participated in the Eucharist for pilgrims in the evening. During the Sign of Peace, I experienced a deeply felt awareness that all these people were my brothers and sisters, every one of them. The awareness continued throughout the ensuing days and weeks that followed. I came to realize, experientially, that every human being is my brother and sister, since we are all a part of the family of God. Those I agree with or disagree with, those who are different from me, those whom I like or do not like—the whole broad spectrum of humanity. This experience expanded my perception of the Church as a whole and my life as a believer.

In these difficult days, when we are besieged by the dreadful revelations of abuse and lies of the Church leadership, by the pain and destruction of lives by large numbers of clerics, religious, and some laypeople, we have to ask these question: What does it mean to be at home in the Church today? How should I be thinking about my Church? How do we respond communally to the nightmare we face? The Church is at a crossroads, perhaps even a breaking point, because of several streams of conflict that have created a perfect storm of deep anger and frustration among the people of God.

Just to enumerate a few of these points of conflict:

- A clergy abuse scandal that has been handled incompetently from the beginning (denial, untruths,

cover-ups, "secret agreements," criminal behavior, lack of professional and capable oversight)
- The polarization of political and ecclesial
issues in society that has prevented a proper
civil discourse on these issues
- Limitations that have been put on women to
prevent them from having an effective voice in
the Church, which translates as them having
no real power or authority in the direction of
the Church in the twenty-first century
- An unwillingness to study and learn more from
social sciences about the mystery of human
sexuality and its ramifications for contemporary human beings (e.g., gay, lesbian, transgen-
der, bisexual, and queer)
- The rise of antireligious fervor and pro-scientism

Patterned ways of thinking or feeling give us a sense of
comfort and control in any particular situation. A dispropor-
tionate and recurring reaction is an invitation to us to change
a behavior. Perhaps this is what we need to see in response to
the multiple scandals in our Church leadership. We are being
invited to change the way that we relate to the hierarchy of
the Church, and the hierarchy is being invited to modify its
stance toward those entrusted to its care. We must interpret
and respond to this ongoing systemic blindness with clarity
and courage. To accept and support clericalism only serves
to encourage an adolescent approach to faith and religion. It
does not help anyone to mature in his or her spiritual journey.
We know that some values are more important than others
are; hence, integrity and truth are more important than repu-
tation and protection of an institutional name.

At Home in the Church

The Catholic Church is not a comfort club. If it feels like weekly visits to the club where everything is predictable, everyone has their part to play, and everyone looks and acts the same, then it's not the Church! The Church is messy because people's lives are messy and unclear—beliefs, attitudes, stories, relationships, and actions are all varied because people come in all shapes and varieties and bring with them all kinds of confusion and complexity. The Church is more akin to a boot camp in that we are immersed in an almost brutal school of learning how to live together in truth and compassion. This means that we must work at growing into persons of integrity and virtue. It involves facing and integrating one's shadow and the shadowy aspects of the community. This double-edged sword includes both the sinister and the golden aspects of people's lives. The shadow is the reservoir of the rejected, denied, and unacceptable parts of one's life. We often project these aspects onto other individuals, groups, and institutions. Reclaiming and integrating this personal energy is difficult, courageous work that is necessary for the process of maturation, both personally and communally. Think of how different the Church would be if this were to happen! So which group of people would you prefer to sit with in the pew for Sunday morning Eucharist? Those who are externally nice and socially acceptable or people who are authentic and "connectable"?

Conflict is a necessary part of human interrelationship and growth. Conflict makes us aware that something is out of alignment and needs to be addressed. Proper respect for the other person is foundational for harmony to exist. This involves respecting other people's thoughts and feelings, finding a real balance to the intellectual and emotional reality of the other person or group. This will include an open-minded and informed attitude toward, for example, masculine and feminine values. This point is often overlooked, especially in the Catholic Church. The denigration of the feminine involves more than simply ignoring the gift of women in Church leadership. It is about disrespecting a way of being and relating in the world.

Another issue that often arises in pastoral counseling and spiritual direction is the matter of dealing with loss. The loss of innocence, self-respect, loss of a loved one, a role, loss of comfort and security in the Church, one's voice, the loss of friendship, or loss of faith in the Church. The Catholic Church claims to be more than human, above all this, but we now know this is not true. These losses all require one thing—the need to eventually accept the unacceptable, and from that point find a way to move forward in life. But what if you do not, or cannot, find that acceptance—what then? Perhaps it might be time to choose a different path or response to the loss. Creatively and imaginatively finding another response is what transforms the trauma of loss into growth.

I remember an older priest friend of mine who was really struggling with the effects of the clergy abuse scandal. He was outraged, deeply saddened, and feeling betrayed by the institution that he had faithfully served for so many years. As we talked, I asked him what he was doing about integrating this pain into his prayer life. He admitted that he had not done much other than to feel his deep loss. I encouraged him to find a way to enter his imagination and really look closely at this negativity. Later, when I met up with him, I asked him how his creative prayer was coming along. He happily replied that he had made some progress in that he had pictured some of the various aspects of his interior life gathered around the altar. This was a good start. However, much later when we talked again, he finally admitted in a much more subdued tone of voice that it was no longer an altar that contained the image of gathering, but a whole room full of personages, both positive and negative! I must admit as my friend grew in accepting these aspects of himself, he became a much more authentic and compassionate human being.

Discipleship is much more than just showing up for Sunday Eucharist. It is about a full, daily immersion in the mystery of the gospel message in good times and tough times. There are four stages to the development of what Pope Francis calls Missionary Discipleship:

1. Pre-evangelization: An environment of welcoming, hospitality, beauty, goodness, and compassion
2. Evangelization: Clear proclamation of the good news that you are truly loved by God
3. Catechesis: Deeper understanding of what the good news means and how to apply it to all aspects of your life
4. Discipleship: A vibrant following of Jesus and a living out of his teachings and values in the details of one's life

One way of developing a deeper, more mature discipleship is by participating in spiritual direction. This is an ancient way of seeking to discern God's guidance with a trained spiritual director, who regularly listens carefully to our life stories, and helps us to make decisions that are in line with our faith. We witness to our faith by the way we live our lives and invite others to hear the good news of Christ. In summary, it is through witness and invitation, through the daily activities of our life, that others may come to know Christ.

Three traditional spiritual practices that help us to deepen an authentic religious commitment are prayer, fasting, and almsgiving. Prayer reminds us of our connection to God; fasting helps us to focus on what is out of order in our life; and the giving of alms reminds us of our connection with the human community. What type of prayer helps you to connect with God? Here are some ideas:

- Meditation
- Music
- Communal prayer
- Reading the psalms
- Spontaneous prayer

What type of fasting helps you to find a better balance in your life? Here are a few examples:

- Fasting from judgmentalism
- Fasting from negativity
- Refraining from using iPhone, iPad, and the like for a period
- Fasting from criticism or gossip
- Fasting from food or liquor for a period

What type of almsgiving will assist you in remembering your relationship to others in the human family? Here are some ways that have helped others: The generous giving of your

- time
- talents
- expertise

- presence to those in need (e.g., tutoring, mentoring, companioning, volunteering, charitable giving, social advocacy)

Another disciplined way of doing this is to watch your language when you speak about "others." Rather than saying *those* strangers or *these* poor homeless or *that* group. Why not practice saying: *our* poor, *our* homeless, or *our* gay and lesbian brothers and sisters? It certainly changes our perspective and reminds us that we do belong to one another.

Jonathon Welch is a wonderful example of someone who has taken the idea of almsgiving to a completely new creative level—literally. He is an Australian musician and opera singer who founded The Choir of Hard Knocks for homeless people in Melbourne. For thirteen years, he has brought otherwise unimaginable joy and community to people for whom the struggles of daily existence were overwhelming. Marginalized, poor, and sometimes suffering from mental health issues, the members of the choir found new hope, new acceptance, and a sense of pride in themselves, thanks to the generosity of Jonathon's almsgiving of his talents, his time, and his resources. He helped them to discover a new way of expressing themselves, forming and strengthening communities in the process.

How do we connect, then, our personal growth with our membership of the Church community? One of the main ways is the symbols and images that the Church holds up for us. The Church offers us deep truths using symbols and images, for it is images that change us much more than mere concepts.

Symbols and images hold a great deal of power for us. They express for us deeper meanings that are often beyond words. This is why we keep and treasure certain gifts or memorabilia for years, even a lifetime. These objects carry for us significance and a reality that belongs to the heart, although their external appearance may not speak to anyone else. They help us to negotiate and articulate our passage through life. To consciously live a symbolic life is to live a religious life. The dynamism is the same. It is intuitively recognizing that reality is infused with the Divine Presence. This is what the incarnation witnesses so emphatically—material and spiritual reality are joined. When we recognize this, we come to reverence all of reality. We "see" God through creation. Is there a symbol or image in your local church that grabs or arrests you, or do you look around and see the "same old, tired, worn out symbols"? Is there an image that challenges you to think or feel differently? Several years ago, I was visiting a church outside Albuquerque, New Mexico. As I entered the foyer, I was stunned by the provocative but beautiful large, wooden statue of the Blessed Virgin Mary as a middle-aged woman, complete with wrinkles and a serious appearance. I was forced to stop and ponder the meaning of her presence in this contemporary form. It was art and symbol at its best!

Liturgy is our most accessible way of carrying symbols. In the Liturgy, we embrace and interact with the symbols—bread, wine, oil, water, and so on—in an active form of worship of God, and we then move to the active engagement of caring for others and stewarding creation. The various seasons of the liturgical year remind us of the mysteries, not only of Christ's life, but also of our own. As we progress in maturity, we notice the positive and healthy repetitive patterns of our lives and uncover a deeper wisdom. The liturgy helps us to make this connection so that we can honor the details of our day-to-day living and feel at home in the Church because the reality of our lives is being mirrored in the action taking place. To discover God's presence in the unfolding mystery of our own lives is the work of a true believer. We are meant to reflect the presence of God in our very being.

Through the Christian viewpoint, this means that we are invited to enter and practice living in the arduous values that Jesus taught and lived:

- Connectedness: We all belong to each other
- Inclusivity: All are welcome at the table
- Forgiveness: All is forgiven, so we forgive others
- Non-judgmentalism: Accepting people as they are
- Creativity: Living from a "both/and" stance to life
- Nonviolence: Building bridges between people and nations
- Wisdom: Living from the interior life of the heart
- Healing: Bringing things into proper balance
- Courage: To challenge injustice
- Authenticity: Living and speaking the truth
- God: Always and everywhere lovingly present

This involves not only observing and changing our behavior, but also our thoughts and attitudes—perhaps the most challenging work of all (see Matt 5:1–48). This is why we are given to each other—to support and encourage one another on the journey to the kingdom. We are mirrors for each other.

The Church is both human and divine. I will say this yet again: The best that it can do is point us in the direction of God. There is an old Latin proverb: "The corruption of the best is the worst." That is certainly true regarding the Church.

The Church at its best has produced saints, mystics, brilliant women and men who have blessed us with magnificent works of art, music, literature, and architecture. Over the period of two thousand years, we have also suffered through some of the most corrupt and sinful leadership that the world has seen. Wars, sexual abuse, embezzlement, illicit liaisons, witch hunts, mismanagement, and other treacheries have been heaped on people, all in the name of God!

The Church is truly a mystery, in that we see only a part of its reality. The unseen, unknown aspect is what motivates us to grapple with the eternally challenging reality of creating a living community of faith-filled disciples. When pondering the mystery of the Church, the late Cardinal Avery Dulles suggested six models to help our understanding of the different facets of the Church: Institution, Sacrament, Herald, Servant, Community, and School of Discipleship. Each of us will find one or more of these models to be a congenial "home" for us within the Church.

Home is where the heart is, but the heart is a fickle creature. It is a great task to recognize that our world and our Church are infinitely bigger than any one of us and that there is room for all. As James Joyce once said of the Catholic Church, "Here comes everybody."

Here's to Everybody!

WORKS CITED

Brueggemann, Walter. 2001. *The Prophetic Imagination*. Minneapolis: Augsburg Fortress.

Cassian, John. 1985. *Conferences*. Classics of Western Spirituality. New York: Paulist Press.

Catechism of the Catholic Church. Our Sunday Visitor 2000.

Chapman, Gary, and Jennifer Thomas. 2006. *Five Languages of Apology: How to Experience Healing in All Your Relationships*. Chicago: Northfield.

Clarke, Jim. 2011. *Creating Rituals: A New Way of Healing for Everyday Life*. Mahwah, NJ: Paulist Press.

————. 2015. *Soul-Centered: Spirituality for People on the Go*. Mahwah, NJ: Paulist Press.

Confraternity of Christian Doctrine. 1970. *The New American Bible*. Encino, CA: Benziger.

Feuerbach, Ludwig. 1989. *Essence of Christianity*. New York: Prometheus Books.

Hollis, James. 1994. *Under Saturn's Shadow: The Wounding and Healing of Men*. Toronto: Inner City Books.

Holloway, Richard. 2008. *Between the Monster and the Saint:*

3/24

The Divided Spirit of Humanity. Melbourne: The Text Publishing Company.

Moore, Robert, and Douglas Gillette. 1990. *King, Warrior, Magician, Lover*. San Francisco: Harper Collins.

Nolan, Albert. 2001. *Jesus Before Christianity*. Maryknoll, NY: Orbis.

Paul VI. 1968. *Humanae Vitae*. http://w2.vatican.va/content/paul-vi/en/encyclicals/documents/hf_p-vi_enc_25071968_humanae-vitae.html.

Piper, Ailsa, and Tony Doherty. 2017. *The Attachment*. N.p.: W. F. Howes Ltd.

Pope Francis. 2015. *Laudato Si'*. http://w2.vatican.va/content/francesco/en/encyclicals/documents/papa-francesco_20150524_enciclica-laudato-si.html.

Rohr, Richard. 2011. *Falling Upward: A Spirituality for the Two Halves of Life*. San Francisco: Jossey Bass.

Rolheiser, Ronald. 2015. *The Passion and the Cross*. Cincinnati: Franciscan Media.

Silverio de Santa Teresa, P. 2003. *Dark Night of the Soul: St. John of the Cross*. Translated by E. Allison Peers. Mineola, NY: Dover.

Windsor, Gerard. 2017. *The Tempest Tossed Church: Being a Catholic Today*. Sydney, NSW: New South Publishing.

Zimmerman, Jack, and Virginia Coyle. 2009. *The Way of Council*. Las Vegas: Bramble Books.